POWER-GLIDE

FOREIGN
LANGUAGE COURSES

Power-Glide Children's French

Parent's Guide

by

Robert W. Blair

with

Dell Blair

This product would not have been possible without the assistance of many people. The help of those mentioned below was invaluable.

Editorial, Design and Production Staff

Instructional Design: Robert Blair, Ph.D., Dell Blair

Project Coordinator: James Blair

Development Manager: Erik D. Holley

Story Writer: Aaron Eastley

Cover Design: Guy Francis

Contributing Editors: Aaron Eastley, Erik D. Holley

Assistant Editors: Krista Halverson, Sean Healy, Ingrid Kellmer

Voices, Audio Cassettes: Jana Adams, Martha Beddoes, Richard DeLong, Björn Farmer, Antje Farmer, Amy LeFevre, Marcie McCarthy, Greg Peterson, Dathan Young

Illustrators: Krista Halverson, Apryl Robertson

Translators: Robert Blair, Dell Blair, Björn Farmer, Antje Farmer, Ingrid Kellmer

Music: SYNTH Sound Recording, Stock-Music.com

Audio Recording, Editing and Mixing: Geoff Groberg

Power-Glide Foreign Language Courses
1682 W 820 N, Provo, UT 84601

Contents

A Note to Parents

Basic Course Objectives

The major goal of this course is to get children excited about communicating in another language. The adventure story, the variety of activities, and the simplified teaching methods employed in the course are all designed to make learning interesting and fun.

This course is primarily for children Kindergarten through 4th grade. Course activities are designed specifically with these learners in mind and include matching games, story telling, speaking, drawing, creative thinking, acting, and guessing—all things which children do for fun!

Ultimately, children who complete the course can expect to understand an impressive amount of French, including several common French phrases, some complete French sentences, French numbers, colors, and body part words, and instructions for drawing and acting given in French. They will also be able to understand stories told all or mostly in French, to retell these stories using French themselves, and to make up stories of their own using words and sentence patterns they have learned.

Children who complete the course will be well prepared to continue learning at a more advanced level, and they will have the foundation that will make learning at that level just as fun and interesting, albeit more challenging than in this course.

Teaching Techniques

This course allows your children to learn by doing: to learn through enjoyable experiences. The idea is to put the experience first and the explanation after. This is important to note because it is directly opposite to how teaching—and especially foreign language teaching—is traditionally done. Typically foreign language teachers spend the majority of their time explaining complex grammar and syntax rules, and drilling students on vocabulary. In this traditional mode, rules and lists come first and experience comes last. Learning experientially, on the other hand, simulates the natural language acquisition process of children.

When children learn their native languages apparently effortlessly in early childhood, it is not through the study of grammar rules and vocabulary lists. Rather, they learn the words for things around them simply by listening to others, and they intuitively grasp an amazing amount of grammar and syntax in the same way.   By using activities that simulate natural language acquisition, it is not only possible, but normal for children to learn a new language quickly and enjoy doing it!

Specifically, this course motivates your children to learn French by providing learning experiences in the form of matching games, story telling exercises, drawing exercises, singing and acting, and other fun activities aimed at developing functional language comprehension and speaking ability. These activities contrast markedly with the exercises in more traditional courses, which tend to focus exclusively on learning some vocabulary, or on understanding very simple French sentences, without extending learning to the point of actually understanding and speaking the language. Significantly as well, the language your children will acquire through this course will be more useful to them than language learned through traditional approaches, because knowledge gained in fun rather than stressful ways is much easier for children to retain and much more natural for them to use themselves.

Using the Course

This course is carefully designed so that it can be used either by children working primarily on their own or by parents and children working closely together. Complete instructions, simple enough to be easily followed by children, are included on the tapes. However, to get the most out of the course, parents should use the thorough written instructions provided in the *Parent's Guide*. The *Parent's Guide* page or pages for each exercise state exercise objectives, provide instructions for students and teaching tips for parents, and give a full audio transcript. Using these helps, parents or other adults can enhance the course significantly by acting as facilitators: reviewing instructions, encouraging creativity and course participation, providing frequent opportunities for children to display what they have learned, rewarding effort and accomplishment, and providing enthusiasm. Keep in mind that much of the real learning takes place as you interact with your children during and after the course learning experiences.

Using the resources provided in the course book and *Parent's Guide*, an adult learning facilitator does not need to know French or how to teach it in order to be a great learning partner. In fact, one of the most enjoyable and effective ways to learn is together, as a team.

Parents or other adults who know French can, of course, supplement the materials in this course very effectively. A proficient bilingual facilitator could, for example: (1) help children learn additional vocabulary by putting several objects on table and asking and answering questions about them, such as "What is this?" or "Where is the _____?", and so on; (2) create on-the-spot diglot-weave stories by reading illustrated children's books, putting key words (picturable nouns) into French, and asking questions about the story or its pictures partly or completely in French; (3) involve children in making and doing things (such as making a paper airplane or finding a hidden object) giving instructions all or partly in French.

Benefits of Second Language Acquisition

Learning a second language has many benefits. Besides the obvious value of being able to understand and communicate with others, research in the United States and Canada in the 1970s and '80s has shown that learning a second language gives children a distinct advantage in general school subject areas. Seeing linguistic and cultural contrasts as they acquire a second language, children gain insight not only into the new language and cultures, but into their own language and culture as well. Furthermore, a considerable amount of research has shown that learning a second language in childhood helps children learn to read and write their native language.

Our Goal

Our goal at Power-Glide is to change the way the U.S. studies language. We want to help people really understand and be able to use foreign languages, not just study them. This *Children's French Course* effectively launches children into understanding and being able to use French. We hope you and your children will find delight in the adventure of learning another language.

Flight to the Island

This section contains an audio transcript of the adventure story your children will hear on the tape.

Instructions for This Page

Have your children listen carefully as the adventure story is read on the tape. Also, encourage your children to take an active part in listening to the adventure story. Ask them to respond to things they hear and have them say out loud words said by the characters on the tape.

 Younger children might enjoy coloring the picture as the adventure story is read. Older children may want to follow along with the written audio transcript provided in this *Parent's Guide*.

Corresponding Page from Children's Activity Book

The Adventure Begins
Flight to the Island

1

Audio Transcript

 Narrator 2: The Adventure Begins: Flight to the Island

Narrator: One winter around Christmas time you are invited by your aunt and uncle to spend a week at a beach house on a small island in the Caribbean. Your aunt and uncle have some business to conduct with people on the island, and they thought it might be fun for you to join their children, your cousins Jenny and Peter, for a week on the beach. You have a long but exciting flight to get there, first in a huge airliner jet, then in a small six seat airplane. The ride in the smaller airplane is really exciting, because you fly just a couple hundred feet over the ocean. As you're flying along, Jenny, who has been looking intently out the window says:

Jenny: Hey look you guys, there are things swimming down there in the water. They don't look like fish to me!

Narrator: And Peter agrees:

Peter: Yeah, they're more round, instead of long like a fish. And they must be really big, for us to see them from up here. What are they?

Narrator: The pilot smiles back at you and, talking loudly to be heard over the thrum of the engine, tells you that they are giant sea turtles, and are very common in this part of the world. "Wow, giant sea turtles!" you exclaim. "This vacation is going to be a real adventure!"

Peter: Yeah. I can't wait to get to where we're staying and go out on the beach, and swim in the ocean!

Jenny: Me neither!

Narrator: You nod your head in agreement as well, but continue looking out your window at the huge sea turtles swimming in the clear blue sea below you. Your aunt and uncle talk with the pilot, sometimes in English and sometimes in French, as you go along.

After another half hour you see an island up ahead. A circle of lovely white sand beaches encircles brilliant green trees that stretch for miles and

Continued from Children's Activity Book, page 1

miles over tall, pointing looking hills. The pilot lands the plain expertly on a rough runway with cows grazing contentedly just off the pavement. You all pile out of the plane and into a waiting taxi that takes you like a flash to the house you'll be staying at on the beach. Dusk is settling in as you arrive, and after your long day of traveling, you all fall asleep soon after eating your dinner.

You all wake up early the next morning, though, and before you even eat breakfast, you, Jenny and Peter run down onto the beach. The sun has only been up for an hour or so, but the sand is already hot.

Jenny: Wow, you guys, the sun is so bright and warm here, even early in the morning.

Peter: Yeah, Jenny, this is lots better than the snow and cold back home. I can't believe that it could be so cold at home but so warm here, at the same time of year!

Jenny: I know. The sand is so hot and soft. But if you dig you feet down into it, it's still cool underneath. It kind of glitters in the sun, too, like there's gold dust in it or something.

Narrator: "Yeah," you agree. "And I can see lots of tiny bits of seashells in it too. Can you guys see them?"

Peter: Uh-ha. And look how clear blue the water is out is the bay! I say we go swimming later.

Jenny: Yeah, me too.

Narrator: You're eager to go swimming yourself, and you look longingly out across the water. Just then, as if it had just materialized out of a mirage, you see something far out in the bay. "Hey, Jenny and Peter," you shout. "Look out there in the bay! There's a boat!"

Jenny: A boat? Oh, yeah, I can see it now too. There's a man and a boy in it.

Peter: I'll bet it's a fishing boat! And look, I think they are coming in! The man is waving to us!

Narrator: "Let's stay here and meet them," you say. "It will be fun to make some new friends. And maybe they can tell us what some good things are to do here."

Peter: I'll bet they could, but how will we understand them, you guys? Dad said most of the people here speak French! Do you guys know any French?

Jenny: Well, only a little. My friend, Marguerite, taught me some.

Peter: Will you teach us what you know? I don't think I know any.

Narrator: "Yeah, me neither," you agree.

Jenny: Well, do you know what a souvenir is, or an éclair?

Peter: Of course we know what those are. But we use those words in English, too. Are they really French words?

Jenny: Yep. And that means you already know some French!

Peter: Great! Teach us more. What things should we say when we meet someone?

Jenny: Well, you can say *bonjour*. That means, "Good day." It's a nice way of saying Hello. And if you're saying goodbye to someone it's *au revoir*.

Peter: *Bonjour. Au revoir.* Okay. And how would I say, "I'm Peter" or "My name's Peter" in French?

Jenny: You mean, how would you say it en *français*?

Peter: Uh, I guess so. Does *en français* mean "in French"?

Jenny: Yes! Nice job, Peter.

Peter: Thanks!

Jenny: Well, let's see. *En français* "I am Peter" would be *Je suis* Peter.

Peter: *Je suis* Peter. That's not too hard to remember. *Je suis* Peter.

Jenny: And to say "I am American" is easy too, it's *Je suis américain*.

Narrator: "*Je suis américain*," you say. "OK. Then how about 'I speak English'"?

Jenny: That's *Je parle anglais. Parle* means "speak" in French.

Continued from Children's Activity Book, page 1

Narrator: "So," you say, "'I speak French'" would be, *'Je parle français,'* right?"

Jenny: Right on!

Narrator: "Hey," you say. "I think I'm getting the hang of this. So how would you ask someone if they speak English then?"

Jenny: *Parlez-vous anglais!*

Peter: *Parlez-vous anglais?*

Jenny: *Oui!*

Peter: Wait. Does "*oui*" mean "yes"?

Jenny: Uh-ha. So when you asked me if *Parlez-vous anglais?* is how you say, "Do you speak English," I replied: "Yes," *Oui.*

Peter: I get it! *Oui.* And what's the word for no?

Jenny: It's *non. Non* means no in French. And to ask somebody if they speak French, can you guess how you would say that?

Peter: Would it be, *Vous parlez français?*

Jenny: *Non. Vous parlez français* means, "You do speak French."

Peter: Oh, right. Then it would be *Parlez-vous français,* right?

Jenny: *Oui!* You switch the words around to make it a question. And if you wanted to ask me *en français* if that was right, you could have said, "It would be *parlez-vous français, n'est-ce pas?*"

Peter: *N'est-ce pas?*

Jenny: That's right! *N'est-ce pas* means "Right?" *en français. Vous parlez bien*—You speak well!

Peter. Thanks a lot! Oh, by the way, how would I say "Thanks a lot" *en français?*

Jenny: It would be, *Merci beaucoup.*

Peter: *Merci beaucoup.*

Jenny: You're welcome!

Narrator: "This is great, Jenny," you say. "But I have just a couple more questions. If I want to know what the French word for something is, how do I ask? Like, if I wanted to ask you how to say 'Please,' how would I do it?"

Jenny: Hmmm... Let me think. Oh, I remember now. To ask how to say something in French you would say, *Comment dit-on...* then whatever the English word is and then *en français.* So you would say, *Comment dit-on* "Please" *en français?*

Peter: OK, let me try. *Comment dit-on* "Please" *en français?*

Jenny: How do you say "Please" *en français?*

Peter: *Oui.*

Jenny: "Please" *en français* is *s'il vous plaît.*

Peter: *S'il vous plaît.* OK. I'll try to remember that. And my last question is, what if somebody uses a French word I don't know? How can I ask them what it means?

Jenny: Oh. That one's longer. You say, *Qu'est-ce que veut dire...?* and then the word. So if I said *bonjour* and you didn't know what that means, you could ask me, *Qu'est-ce que veut dire "bonjour"?* and I would tell you, *Bonjour* means "Hello" or "Good day"!

Narrator: "That one is a bit trickier," you say. "*Qu'est-ce que veut dire...* It kind of sounds like CASK OF A DEER, doesn't it?"

Jenny: *Oui,* it does! You guys are doing great! It took me a long time to learn those words from Marguerite.

Peter: Merci!

Narrator: "Yeah, thanks again, Jenny," you say. "And look, you guys, "The fishermen are almost here!"

Jenny: Do you want to learn any more?

Peter: *Non.* I think maybe we should just review what we've learned so far. Then you can teach us more words later.

Jenny: OK. That's about all I know anyway!

Narrator: So instead of learning any more new words for now, you and Peter take a few minutes while the fishermen are still rowing toward the shore to review what Jenny has taught you.

Familiar Phrases

This activity lets your children see how many of the French words and phrases from the adventure story they can remember. The narrator will read through the words and phrases twice, reading the French and then pausing for your children to say the English equivalent before giving the translation. Reading through twice will allow your children to review any words they don't remember during the first read through, and still be able to give the correct translation the second time.

Instructions for This Page

Have your children look at the French phrases in their activity books as they are read on the tape. During the pause after each French word or phrase is read, have your children say the English translation out loud.

 If your children cannot remember some of the words, or give the wrong translation the first time through, simply let them listen to the correct answers given on the tape and try again during the second reading. If they still miss more than one or two on the second read through, let them rewind the tape and complete the entire activity again, with your help.

Audio Transcript

Narrator 2: Activity: Familiar Phrases.

Narrator: Let's review the new words and phrases. As I say the words in French, try to say the right English words out loud. For example, if I were to say *bonjour*, you would say "Good day" out loud. OK? Let's try a few.

1. *Bonjour.* Did you say, "Good day"? Good!

Corresponding Page from Children's Activity Book

🔊

Familiar Phrases

1. *Bonjour.*	Good day.
2. *Au revoir.*	Goodbye.
3. *Je suis.*	I am.
4. *Je parle anglais.*	I speak English.
5. *S'il vous plaît.*	Please.
6. *Parlez-vous français?*	Do you speak French?
7. *Oui.*	Yes.
8. *Non.*	No.
9. *N'est-ce pas?*	Right?
10. *Merci beaucoup.*	Thanks a lot.

2

2. *Au revoir.* Did you say, "Goodbye"? Very good.

3. *Je suis.* It's, "I am", right?

4. *Je parle anglais.* You should have said, "I speak English."

5. *S'il vous plaît.* Did you say, "Please"? Good!

6. *Parlez-vous français?* Did you say, "Do you speak French?" Good.

7. *Oui.* Did you say, "Yes"? Good.

8. *Non.* Did you say, "No"? Good.

9. *N'est-ce pas?* Did you say, "Right?" Good.

10. *Merci beaucoup.* Did you say, "Thanks a lot"? Well done.

Were you able to say the correct English words? Good work! Let's go through the French words and phrases one more time. This time I'll just say the French words followed by the English words.

1. *Bonjour.* "Good day."

Continued from Children's Activity Book, page 2

2. *Au revoir.* "Goodbye."

3. *Je suis.* "I am."

4. *Je parle français.* "I speak English."

5. *S'il vous plaît.* "Please."

6. *Parlez-vous français?* "Do you speak French?"

7. *Oui.* "Yes."

8. *Non.* "No."

9. *N'est-ce pas?* "Right?"

10. *Merci beaucoup.* "Thanks a lot."

How did you do that time? Better? Great! Now, let's go on with the adventure.

Meeting Derek and Pierre

This section contains an audio transcript of the adventure story your children will hear on the tape.

Instructions for This Page

Have your children listen carefully as the adventure story is read on the tape. Also, encourage your children to take an active part in listening to the adventure story. Ask them to respond to things they hear and have them say out loud words said by the characters on the tape.

 Younger children might enjoy coloring the picture as the adventure story is read. Older children may want to follow along with the written audio transcript provided in this *Parent's Guide*.

When your children get to the part of the adventure story where Derek makes quiche lorraine, stop the tape and turn to the Recipes section at the back of this *Parent's Guide* to find the recipe. Try making some!

Audio Transcript

 Narrator 2: The Adventure Continues: Meeting Derek and Pierre.

Narrator: Just as you finish going over the words and phrases you've learned, the fishermen arrive. Now that they are much closer you can see that one of them is a man, and the other a teenager, or maybe even a boy, about your age. Once they are close enough to hear you Jenny calls out:

Jenny: *Bonjour!*

Narrator: And the fisherman calls back heartily:

Derek: *Bonjour!*

Peter: *Bonjour! Je suis* Peter!

Corresponding Page from Children's Activity Book

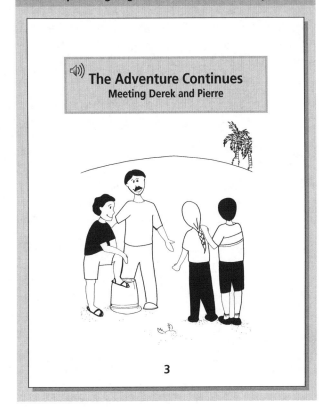

Jenny: *Et je suis* Jenny!

Narrator: You call out your name as well, and the man and the boy, after pulling their boat up on to the dry sand, come over to meet you. The man introduces himself first.

Derek: *Je suis* Derek.

Pierre: *Et je suis* Pierre. *Enchanté de faire votre connaissance.*

Peter: What? I don't understand.

Derek: *Parlez-vous français?*

Jenny: *Non.* Or at least, only a little. *Parlez-vous anglais?*

Derek: Yes, I speak English. And my nephew, Pierre, here, does too.

Pierre: Pretty well, anyway. Uncle Derek has taught me. But most of the people here only speak French.

Continued from Children's Activity Book, page 3

Jenny: We know. We're only visiting your island for a week, but we're hoping to learn a lot more while we're here. In fact, we were just going over a few of the words I already know while we waited for you to row in.

Narrator: "Yeah," you say. "And some of the French words even sound kind of like English words—words like *'souvenir'* and *'éclair.'* It's a really fun language to speak!"

Derek: French is a wonderful language. And you say you want to learn it? That's wonderful indeed! I think I can help you find the treasure you seek.

Peter: Treasure? Is there treasure on this island?

Derek: There is. And not only the kind you're thinking of. But, say, my friends, have you had breakfast yet?

Peter: Well, no.

Derek: Wonderful. You shall join Pierre and me. We always have a big breakfast after our morning fishing. I'll make us all a fine *quiche lorraine*, I think, and you'll enjoy the fruits we have here on

l'île as well. And also, I think, while we eat I'll help you begin on your quest for the treasure.

Narrator: "That does sound delicious!" you say.

Peter: And exciting!

Derek: Very good. Let's all walk up to my home, then. It's just there, at the top of the beach.

Narrator: You, Jenny and Peter now notice a fine looking beach house nestled just inside the coconut trees at the top of the beach. Two long fishing boats like the one Derek and Pierre were out in a few moments ago are resting upside down out in front of the house. Soon you are all seated around a table on Derek's front porch, enjoying a scrumptious breakfast of quiche lorraine, bananas, mangoes, papayas and passion fruit drinks.

As you eat, Derek offers to tell you a short story.

Jenny: That sounds great, Derek. I love stories!

Derek: Good! This story I have to tell you is about a little girl and a rat.

Match and Learn

Match and Learn
Point to what you hear

4

This activity is visual, audio, and kinesthetic. It is designed to help your children learn by listening and pointing.

This first activity introduces the match and learn frames used frequently in this course.

Instructions for This Page

Have your children point to the picture as the tape directs.

 Younger children might enjoy coloring the pictures as the French words are said. Encourage your children to use these new words whenever possible. Make flash-cards of the various pictures with the French words on the back and test your children regularly. Have your children create stories similar to the narrator's story at the end of the activity using these new vocabulary words.

Roche... Of course, since the other box is empty, you point to the rock.

Audio Transcript

Narrator 2: Activity: Match and Learn.

Narrator: Here are the things Derek teaches you. First, as you already know, some French words sound a lot like English words. For example, the English word "rock" sounds a lot like the French word *roche.* Listen again, you can hear how close they are: rock...*roche.*

Another word that sounds almost the same in English and French is the word for soup. The French word for soup is *soupe.* Just by knowing the English word soup, you could probably guess what the French word *soupe* means.

One of the ways you can show that you understand words is by pointing to pictures when you hear words. Let's try it. Look at the picture boxes in your activity book and point to what you hear.

Match and Learn

This activity builds on the previous one, continuing the introduction to match and learn picture frames.

Instructions for This Page

Have your children look at the pictures in the frames in their activity books and point to the appropriate objects as directed by the tape.

Audio Transcript

Narrator: There are two frames, or sets of boxes, on this page. The top frame has two boxes with the number 1 to the left of them. In frame 1 you have two choices. You have to choose between two pictures. Listen and point to the picture of the word you hear. Remember we're only looking at the two boxes in frame 1 right now.

In frame one, point to the *soupe*. Did you point to the soup? Good! *Soupe* is the French word for soup. And what is the other picture of? A rock? That's right! Do you remember the French word for rock? It's easy, isn't it? It's just *roche*. Say it out loud, *roche*. Good job.

Now look at the boxes in frame 2 and point to what you hear. *Balle.* You know it's not the *soupe*, the soup, so it must be the ball, right? Good job. The French word for "ball" is *balle*.

Corresponding Page from Children's Activity Book

5

Match and Learn

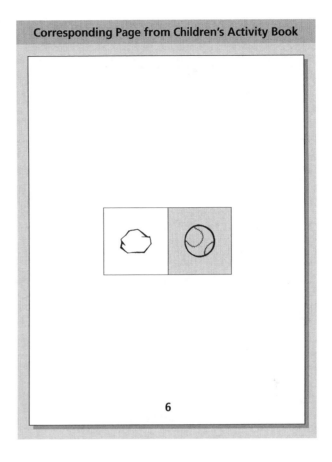

6

This activity builds on the previous one, continuing the introduction to match and learn picture frames.

Instructions for This Page

Have your children look at the pictures in the frame in their activity books and point to the appropriate objects as directed by the tape.

Audio Transcript

Narrator: Here is another frame. Point to what you hear.

Roche… Did you choose the rock? Good! But what is the other picture? Is it a *balle*? That's right!

Now even with only these few words I can tell you a short story using some French. See if you can understand it.

Once upon a time a l child was playing outside with a *balle*. The child's mother said, "The *soupe* is ready, come inside!" "Okay, mom, but I can't find my *balle*. Can you help me find my *balle*?" The mother went to help her child find the *balle*, and she found it behind a great big *roche*. Then they both went inside and ate *soupe*.

A Little Puzzle

This activity uses a puzzle to help your children become more familiar with the vocabulary words they learned in the previous activity.

Instructions for This Page

Have your children listen to the tape and point to the objects as the tape directs.

 Encourage your children to make sentences and comments much like the Narrator does, using the French vocabulary in the puzzle.

Audio Transcript

 Narrator: Now that you're familiar with frames, let's try a little puzzle. Listen and point to the words you hear.

First, point to the *soupe*. It's in the top white box, right? Good! Now point to the *balle*. It's in the bottom gray box, right? Yes. Now point to the *roche*. The *roche* is in the top gray box, right? Good work.

Now point to the *chaussure*. The what? The *chaussure*. You don't know what a *chaussure* is? You know what a *roche* is, right? And you know what *soupe* is, right? And you know what a *balle* is, right? Well, there is only one other picture in the boxes. The shoe? Yes, the *chaussure*. Point to the *chaussure*. It's in the bottom white box, right? Yes.

Corresponding Page from Children's Activity Book

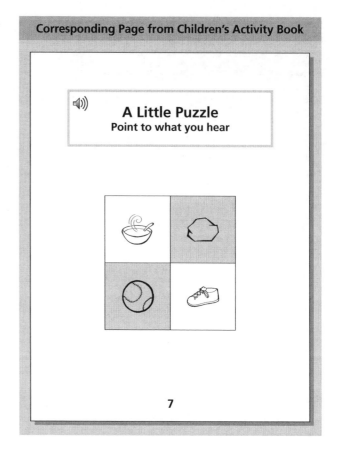

A Little Puzzle
Point to what you hear

7

A Girl and a Rat

Although it is important for children to first understand spoken language, it is exciting when they begin to use it, and that is where the learning really takes off. In this and the following activities we continue with comprehension building, but as the activity progress, we gradually introduce conversation.

Your children will hear a simple story about a girl and a rat several times. They will learn the character names and identify them with pictures. By the time we get to them telling the story, they will have learned to recognize the pictures well enough that they can tell the story simply by looking at them. This builds fluency because they not only go beyond simple comprehension to actual production, but they think in French as they tell the story.

You'll notice that the story is told with a minimum number of words, and in very short, incomplete sentences (Girl sees rat. Rat sees girl., etc.). We do this to simplify communication and pattern it after how children begin communicating in their first language. For example, children say "water" when they mean, "I'm thirsty, please give me water." The same idea holds true in this and other similar activities. We'll start with the most basic communication structure and build from there. Eventually, we'll teach language for more complete sentences.

Instructions for This Page

Have your children look at the illustration for the story "A Girl and a Rat" and listen to the introduction to the story on the tape.

 Make sure your children understand each new French word introduced in the story. For those children who can read and write, teach them to spell each French word.

A Girl and a Rat
Une Histoire

8

Audio Transcript

 Narrator 2: Activity: A Girl and a Rat.

Narrator: Now that you know a few French words, and have learned about frames, I can tell you a story—*une histoire*. I'll tell it to you with some English *mots* (words) *et some* French *mots*. I'll put in *mots français* only when you can easily guess what those *mots* mean.

My *histoire* is very short. It's about a little girl, *une fille*, and a rat, *un rat*. Even though *ma histoire* is very short, you can learn something about life from this *histoire*.

Figure out why the *fille* in the *histoire* laughs, but *le rat* cries. I call *ma* little *histoire* "A Girl and a Rat." *En français* I call it *"Une fille et un Rat."*

Match and Learn

This activity is visual, audio, and kinesthetic. It is designed to help your children learn by listening and pointing.

Instructions for This Page

Have your children point to the correct boxes and pictures as directed by the tape. In the second part of the activity, have them answer out loud the questions asked about the numbered pictures.

Audio Transcript

 Narrator: Before I tell you the *histoire*, I'll teach you some new words to help you understand. Look at the frame with the white and shaded boxes.

Point to the girl, *la fille*. *La fille* is in the top white box, right? Yes. Now point to *le rat*. *Le rat* is in the bottom shaded box, right? Now point to the bear, *l'ours*. Is *l'ours* in the top shaded box? No, *l'ours* is in the bottom white box, right? Now point to the boy, *le garçon*. He is in the top shaded box, right? Good.

Now, see if you can answer some questions about the words you just learned. Look at the picture with the number one next to it.

Number 1. Is this *une fille*? … Yes, it is.

Number 2. Is this *un rat*? … Yes, it is.

Number 3. Is this *une fille* or *le garçon*? … Did you say *une fille*? Yes, it is a girl, it is *une fille*.

Number 4. Is this *une fille* or *un ours*? This is a bear, *un ours*.

Number 5. Is this *un garçon*? … Yes, this is a boy, *un garçon*.

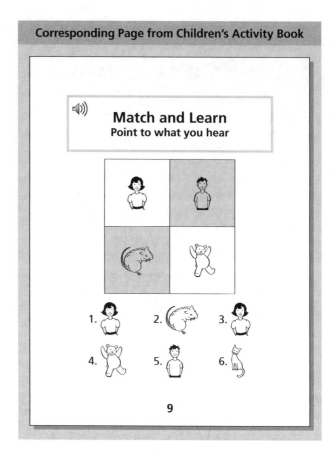

Number 6. Is this *un rat*? … No, this isn't a rat, this is a cat, *un chat*! Good.

Match and Learn

This activity uses the system of frames and numbered pictures learned in the previous activity. A few new French words are introduced.

Instructions for This Page

Have your children point to the correct pictures as the tape instructs. In the second part of the activity, they should answer out loud the questions asked about the numbered pictures.

 As these activities become progressively more challenging, the main objective is to help your children feel confident. They should not be overly concerned with correctness. Encourage them to point boldly as soon as they hear what to point to in the first part of the activity, and to speak out loud in response to the questions in the second half. When your children guess wrong, let them know it's okay and to keep making their best guesses.

Audio Transcript

 Narrator: You did very well with those pictures and words. Let's try a few more. Look at the frame with the white and gray boxes.

Point to *le garçon*. *Le garçon* is in the top gray box, right? Yes. Now, point to the cat, *le chat*. Is *le chat* in the top white box? Yes, *le chat*, the cat, is in the top white box. Point to the tiger, *le tigre*. *Le tigre* is in the bottom white box, right? Now, point to *le rat*. *Le rat* is in the bottom gray box, right? Yes.

Now, see if you can answer some questions about the words you just learned. Look at the picture with the number one next to it.

Number 1. Is this *un chat* or *un rat*? It is *un rat*.

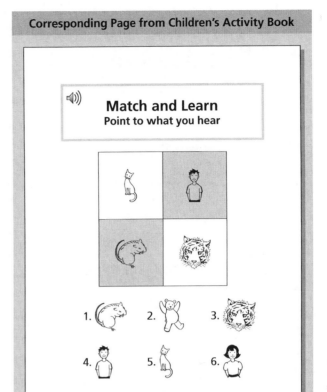

Corresponding Page from Children's Activity Book

Match and Learn
Point to what you hear

1. 2. 3.

4. 5. 6.

10

Number 2. Is this *une fille* or *un ours*? This is *un ours*, a bear.

Number 3. Is this *un tigre*? Yes, it is.

Number 4. Is this *un chat* or *un garçon*? This is *un garçon*.

Number 5. Is this *un rat*? No, it is not *un rat*. It is *un chat*, right?

Number 6. Is this *un garçon* or *une fille*? It's not a boy. It is *une fille*.

Diglot Weave

This activity contains a simple bilingual or diglot weave narrative built around two of the characters from the previous activities. This type of narrative was originally introduced by Professor Rudy Lentulay of Bryn Mawr University as a language learning aid.

Instructions for This Page

Have your children listen carefully and follow the story in their activity books as it is told on the tape.

 Have your children follow the words and pictures of the story with their finger, so that when the tape says the French word for "girl," for instance, their finger is pointing to the picture of the girl. This kinesthetic connection will enhance their mental connections between the French words and the ideas they represent. Once they feel comfortable with this diglot weave, have your children come up with a diglot weave of their own.

Audio Transcript

 Narrator: Now listen as I tell *l'histoire* about *une fille et un rat.* Follow along and look at the pictures.

Une fille sees *un rat. Le rat* sees *la fille. Le rat* squeaks "eek!" *La fille* squeaks back "eek!" *Le rat* runs. *La fille* chases *le rat*, but *le rat* escapes. *La fille* sits down *et* laughs "hee-hee-hee." *Le rat* sits down *et* cries "boo-hoo."

Did you like *ma histoire*? Did you understand all the words? I'll tell *une histoire* one more time and then ask you some questions about it.

Une fille sees *un rat. Le rat* sees *la fille. Le rat* squeaks "eek!" *La fille* squeaks back "eek!" *Le rat*

Corresponding Page from Children's Activity Book

> ### Diglot Weave
> *Une Fille et un Rat*
>
> *Une* 🧒 sees *un* 🐁 . *Le* 🐁 sees
>
> la 🧒 . *Le* 🐁 squeaks "eek!" *La*
>
> 🧒 squeaks back "eek!" *Le* 🐁 runs.
>
> La 🧒 chases *le* 🐁, but *le* 🐁
>
> escapes. *La* 🧒 sits down *et* laughs
>
> "hee-hee-hee." *Le* 🐁 sits down *et*
>
> cries "boo-hoo."
>
> **11**

runs. *La fille* chases *le rat*, but *le rat* escapes. *La fille* sits down *et* laughs "hee-hee-hee." *Le rat* sits down *et* cries "boo-hoo."

Now, I'll ask you some questions. Say your answers out loud. Did *la fille* see a bear, *un ours*? No. Did *un ours* see *un rat*? No! Did *le rat* see *une fille*? Yes! Did *le rat* run? Yes. Did *la fille* chase *le rat*? Yes. Did *le rat* laugh? No. Did *la fille* cry? No.

Match and Learn

This activity uses frames to introduce new pictures in the story. This time there are two pictures in each box instead of one, thereby increasing the difficulty of the activity.

Instructions for This Page

Have your children point to the correct pictures as the tape instructs.

Audio Transcript

 Narrator: Before I tell this *histoire* again, I'll teach you some more words and pictures.

Look at frame 1. Point to the box with the girl and the running legs. Did you point to the top white box? Good. The running legs mean "runs." Together, the pictures in this box mean "girl runs." Now, point to the box with only the girl. The girl is in the bottom gray box. Point to "rat runs." "Rat runs" is in the top gray box. Now point to "boy runs." Did you point to the bottom white box? Good.

Now, look at frame 2. Point to *le rat*. *Le rat* is in the top gray box, right? Now, point to "bear roars." "Bear roars" is in the top white box. See the two pictures: the bear and the roar? This means "bear roars." Point to "rat runs." Did you point to the bottom gray box? Good. Now point to "rat squeaks." "Rat squeaks" is in the bottom white box. Do you see the two pictures: the rat and the eek? This means "rat squeaks."

Let's look now at frame 3. Point to "girl squeaks." Did you point to the top white box? Good. Now, point to "bear roars." "Bear roars" is in the bottom white box. Point to "rat runs." Did you point to the top gray box? Good. Now, point to "girl runs." "Girl runs" is in the bottom gray box, right?

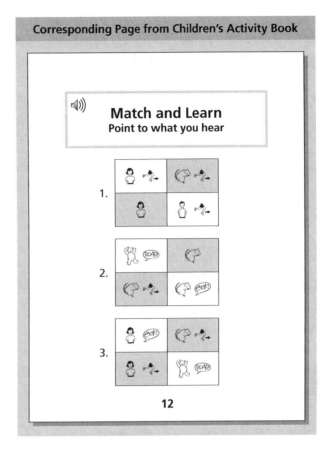

Match and Learn

This activity uses frames once again to introduce more new pictures that can be incorporated into the telling of the story. And once again, this activity is slightly more challenging than the previous one because it contains some boxes with as many as three pictures to identify.

Instructions for This Page

Have your children point to the correct pictures as the tape instructs.

Audio Transcript

 Narrator: Now let's learn the French words for the pictures you just learned.

Look at frame 4. Point to "girl sees rat." "Girl sees rat" is in the top white box. See the three pictures: the girl, the eye, and the rat? Together, the pictures in this box mean "girl sees rat." In French it would be, *fille voit rat*. Now, point to "rat runs," or *rat court. Rat court* is in the bottom gray box, right? Point to "*rat voit fille.*" Did you point to the top gray box? Good. Now, point to *fille poursuit,* or "girl chases." "*fille poursuit*" is in the bottom white box, right? Good.

Now, look at frame 5. Point to *rat pleure,* "rat cries." "Rat cries" is in the top white box, right? Now, point to "rat squeaks," or *rat fait couic.* Did you point to the bottom white box? Good. Now point to "girl laughs," *fille rit. Fille rit* is in the top gray box. Now, point to *rat s'échappe.* Did you point to the bottom gray box? Good.

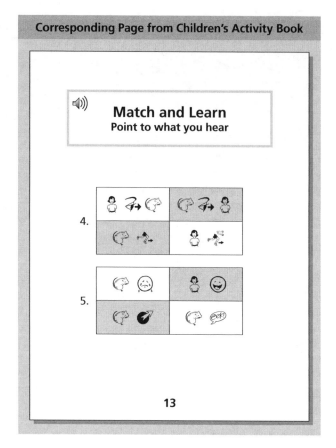

Corresponding Page from Children's Activity Book

◀))

Match and Learn
Point to what you hear

4.

5.

13

Rebus Story

This activity is designed to help your children begin to think in French. This is accomplished by having pictures in their activity books represent the French words read on the tape. This way your children will associate the French words with their English equivalents.

Instructions for This Page

Have your children follow the pictures with their finger as the French words for those pictures are read on the tape.

 This is a good activity for drawing pictures and creating flashcards. Encourage your children to create stories of their own!

Audio Transcript

Narrator: Now that you know the story, try to follow the pictures as I tell you the story all in French. See if you can figure out what they mean. Are you ready? Good! Here we go!

Fille voit rat. Rat voit fille. Rat fait couic. Fille fait couic. Rat court. Fille poursuit rat. Rat s'échappe. Fille rit. Rat pleure.

Were you able to follow along? Could you tell that *s'échappe* means to escape, and that *rit* means to laugh and *pleure* means to cry? Good!

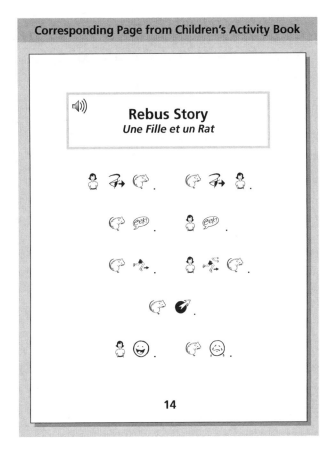

Describe What You See

This activity requires your children to use the French words they learned in the previous activity to describe the pictures they see.

Instructions for This Page

Have your children say the French words for the pictures, or write them on the blank lines to the side of the pictures.

Have your children say or write in as many of the French words as they can on their own. Then you may go back through with them and help them remember those they missed. Continue to encourage them to guess when they need to, and to not feel bad when they cannot remember all the words or when they get one wrong.

Audio Transcript

Narrator: On this page are some of the pictures you have learned the words for. Say the French words for the pictures. Or if you like, write the French words for the pictures in the blanks.

Story Telling

This activity lets your children use the French words they have learned to tell the story of "A Girl and a Rat" themselves.

Instructions for This Page

Have your children follow the trail of pictures (from top to bottom) with their finger, telling the story using the French words for the pictured items as they go.

If your children cannot remember a particular word, let them think for a moment, and then go ahead and help them. Your goal here is to encourage them to think as hard as they can on their own, while keeping them from getting frustrated or discouraged. Encourage them to create their own stories using the pictures in this activity.

Audio Transcript

Narrator: Follow the trail of pictures from top to bottom with your finger, telling the story using the French words for the pictures.

Corresponding Page from Children's Activity Book

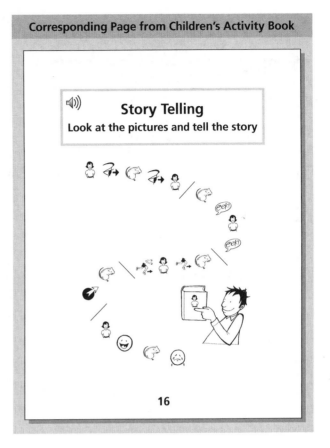

Story Telling
Look at the pictures and tell the story

16

Practice in French

The following activity begins with the story of "A Girl and a Rat" read entirely in French.

This activity then asks your children to tell the story entirely in French on their own, using the pictures in the circle below the French text as memory prompts.

Instructions for This Page

First have your children follow the French text in their activity books as it is read on the tape.

Then have them cover the French text, look at the pictures in the circle below the text, and try to tell the story in French on their own. Record how long it takes them to tell the complete story in French their first time, and then record their best subsequent time.

 Let your children try telling the story as many as six or eight times, perhaps even looking back at the French text on the top of the page and learning the French articles and other connecting words found there. Have them rearrange the sentences, thereby creating their own story.

Audio Transcript

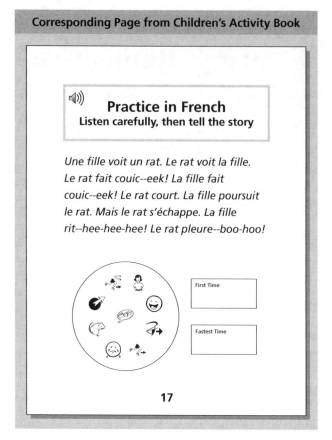

Narrator: Last of all, here is *l'histoire* all in perfect *français*. Listen carefully.

Une fille voit un rat. Le rat voit la fille. Le rat fait couic--eek! La fille fait couic--eek! Le rat court. La fille poursuit le rat. Mais le rat s'échappe. La fille rit--hee-hee-hee! Le rat pleure--boo-hoo!

Were you able to follow along and understand? Good!

A Treasure Map!

This section contains an audio transcript of the adventure story your children will hear on the tape.

Instructions for This Page

Have your children listen carefully as the adventure story is read on the tape. Encourage your children to take an active part in listening to the adventure story. Ask them to respond to things they hear and have them say out loud words said by the characters on the tape.

 Younger children might enjoy coloring the picture as the adventure story is read. Older children may want to follow along with the written audio transcript provided in this *Parent's Guide.*

Audio Transcript

 Narrator 2: The Adventure Continues: A Treasure Map!

Peter: That was a good story, Derek. And it was cool to be able to understand it even when you told it in French.

Narrator: "Yeah," you agree. "We learned some good words, too. This is fun!"

Derek: I'm glad you liked my story. I am very impressed with your desire to learn. In fact, I think you have what it will take to find the treasure of our island.

Narrator: With that, Derek takes a map of the island out of a drawer and places it on the table.

Derek: Here you are, my friends, a map that will help you find the treasure of our island.

Jenny. Oh, wow! A treasure map!

Peter: Yeah, but this isn't like treasure maps I've read about. Instead of one "X" on it, there are lots of black dots, and there are things written on it that I don't understand. Do we have to find all those places with dots by them in order to get the treasure?

Derek: You do. You'll find parts of the treasure you seek at each spot on the map. And some of the writing on the map is French. You'll need to learn what it means along your way. For now, I'll give you your first clue, the first part of your treasure. I give it to you because you have already discovered it on your own. It is: Build on what you already know.

Jenny: Build on what you already know?

Derek: Yes. Just like you all did when you received a couple of French words that are the same in English: *souvenir* and *éclair!*

Peter: Hmm. OK. Build on what you know. That's easy to remember, even if we don't know yet how it will help us find the treasure.

Continued from Children's Activity Book, page 19

Derek: Very good, Peter. Just remember the clues as you go along, and you'll find the treasure in the end. It is a magnificent treasure indeed!

Narrator: "It sounds exciting!" you say. "Maybe we should start by learning the words for the shapes on this map, so we can ask people how to find the places."

Derek: That's an excellent idea. I'll teach you the French words for lines and shapes, and I'll introduce you to a few numbers while we're at it. How does that sound?

Jenny: It sounds fun, Derek!

Peter: Yeah!

Lines and Figures

The following activity is a learning game that uses pictures to help your children learn some new words. The activity is deliberately simple in order to help your children develop confidence in their ability to comprehend a foreign language.

Instructions for This Page

Have your children look at the pictures in their activity books and point to the shapes as they hear the words for those shapes read on the tape. The narrator will read each word twice in French, then go back through the words in French one by one, and finally read the French words all together.

 Help your children identify the right shapes during the first part of the activity (when each new word is read twice). Then let them try pointing on their own after that.

Have your children pause the tape as needed to have time to give their answers.

Audio Transcript

 Narrator 2: Activity: Lines and Figures.

Narrator: Here on your activity book page are the things Derek teaches you about.

Point to what you hear. Circle...*cercle, cercle.* Square...*carré, carré.* Line...*ligne, ligne.* Triangle...*triangle, triangle.*

Did you point to them all? Good job! Now let's go through them once more, in French only.

Point to what you hear.

Triangle, carré, cercle, ligne. Did you point to them all? Good job!

Corresponding Page from Children's Activity Book

◁)) **Lines and Figures**
Point to what you hear

carré

cercle

ligne

triangle

20

Look and Listen

This activity uses the shapes from the previous page in several different combinations.

Learning to identify more than one of the same shape (two circles or three lines, for instance) and various shapes grouped together will give your children added confidence.

Instructions for This Page

Have your children look at the numbered pictures of shapes and sets of shapes in their activity books as the words for those shapes are read on the tape.

 Encourage your children to point to each shape with their finger and count when appropriate as the words are read on the tape. For example, on number 12 they could point to the two squares one by one immediately after "*deux carrés*" is read on the tape, then point to the line as "*et une ligne*" is read on the tape.

Audio Transcript

 Narrator: On this page, point to what you hear.

Number 1. *Cercle*...circle. *Un cercle*.

Number 2. *Carré*...square. *Un carré*.

Number 3. *Triangle*...triangle. *Un triangle*.

Number 4. *Ligne*...line. *Une ligne*.

Number 5. *Un triangle et un carré*. One triangle and one square.

Number 6. *Un cercle et un triangle*. One circle and one triangle.

Number 7. *Deux cercles*. Two circles.

Corresponding Page from Children's Activity Book

◁)))
Look and Listen

1. ○   7. ○○

2. □   8. ○○○ △△

3. △   9. □□ ///

4. /   10. ○○△

5. △□   11. /// ○

6. ○△   12. □□ /

21

Number 8. *Trois cercles et deux triangles*. Three circles and two triangles.

Number 9. *Deux carrés et trois lignes*. Two squares and three lines.

Number 10. *Deux cercles et un triangle*. Two circles and one triangle.

Number 11. *Trois lignes et un cercle*. Three lines and one circle.

Number 12. *Deux carrés et une ligne*. Two squares and one line.

Well done.

Point to What You Hear

This time the shapes will be read in French only. This activity builds the same identification skills as the previous activity, and also reviews the basic French numbers.

Instructions for This Page

As before, have your children look at the pictures in their activity books and point to the shapes and sets of shapes as they hear the French numbers and words for those shapes read on the tape. Then encourage them to call out the French words before they are read on the tape.

Audio Transcript

Narrator: Now look and listen again. This time I'll say just the French names of the shapes, and I'll mix up the order. You point to the shapes that you hear. Ready? OK.

Point to *deux cercles*. It's number 7, right?

Now point to *un triangle*. It's number 3, right?

Now point to *deux carrés et une ligne*. It's number 12, right?

Now point to *deux carrés et trois lignes*. It's number 9, right?

Now point to *une ligne*. It's number 4, right?

Now point to *un cercle*. It's number 1, right?

Now point to *un triangle et un carré*. It's number 5, right?

Now point to *trois lignes et un cercle*. It's number 11, right?

Now point to *un carré*. It's number 2, right?

Now point to *trois cercles et deux triangles*. It's number 8, right?

Now point to *un cercle et un triangle*. It's number 6, right?

And last of all, point to *deux cercles et un triangle*. It's number 10, isn't it?

Were you able to point to most of them? Very well done.

Corresponding Page from Children's Activity Book

Point to What You Hear

1. ○
2. □
3. △
4. /
5. △□
6. ○△

7. ○○
8. ○○○ △△
9. □□ ///
10. ○○△
11. /// ○
12. □□ /

22

Match and Learn

This activity is visual, audio, and kinesthetic. It is designed to help your children learn by listening and pointing.

Instructions for This Page

Have your children look at the pictures in each numbered frame in their activity books and point to the box which contains the shapes whose names are read on the tape. The entire first frame will be read; thereafter, the names for the shapes in three of the four boxes will be read before the tape goes on to the next frame. This will allow for a process of elimination to take place as your children go through the boxes in each numbered frame.

 If it's helpful or fun, encourage your children to mark off the boxes already selected as they go along.

Audio Transcript

 Narrator: Now let's do some match and learn activities. Point to what you hear.

Look at frame 1. Point to *un cercle*. It's in the bottom white box, right? Good. Now point to *deux triangles*. It's in the top white box, right? Now point to *un triangle*. It's the bottom gray box. Now point to *deux cercles*. It's the top gray box, right?

Now look at frame 2. Point to the box with *deux cercles*. It's the top gray box, right? Now point to *deux triangles*. It's the bottom gray box. Now point to *deux lignes*. It's the top white box, right?

Now look at frame 3. Point to the *carré*. It's the top white box, right? Now point to *deux carrés*. It's the top gray box, isn't it? Now point to *une ligne*. It's the bottom white box, right? Well done!

Match and Learn
Point to what you hear

1.
2.
3.
4.
5.
6.

23

Now look at frame 4. Point to *deux triangles*. It's the bottom white box, right? Now point to *un carré et un triangle*. It's the bottom gray box, right? Now point to *un triangle et une ligne*. It's the top white box, right?

Now look at frame 5. Point to *deux lignes et un triangle*. It's the bottom gray box. Now point to *deux cercles et un carré*. It's the bottom white box. Now point to *deux lignes et un carré*. It's the top gray box, right? Yes.

Now look at frame 6. Point to *un cercle, deux triangles et un carré*. It's the bottom white box, isn't it? Now point to *un cercle, deux carrés et une ligne*. It's the top gray box. Now point to *un carré et un cercle*. It's the top white box, right? Well done.

Listen and Draw

After your children develop their ability to comprehend, they'll begin to produce. This activity reinforces their ability to comprehend by having your children do something kinesthetic and creative: drawing what is heard. Drawing helps your children internalize what is being learned because they will have to interpret what is heard in a creative form.

Instructions for This Page

Have your children listen to the descriptions of sets of shapes read on the tape and draw what they hear. These will be combinations of multiple numbers of the same shapes and various other shapes (for instance, number 1 calls for "Two lines and one circle"). Have your children draw all of the shapes for each number in the gray "chalkboard" box next to that number.

Have your children pause the tape as needed to have time to give their answers.

Audio Transcript

 Narrator: These chalkboards are for you to draw on. You'll be drawing squares, *carrés*; circles, *cercles*; triangles, *triangles*; and lines, *lignes*.

I'll name the shapes and you draw them. You can turn off the tape while you get something to write with if you need to. Are you ready? OK. Here we go.

Number 1. *Deux lignes et un cercle. Deux lignes et un cercle.* Two lines and one circle.

Number 2. *Deux cercles et une ligne. Deux cercles et une ligne.* Two circles and one line.

Number 3. *Une ligne, un carré, un cercle, et un triangle. Une ligne, un carré, un cercle, et un trian-*

Corresponding Page from Children's Activity Book

Listen and Draw

1.

2.

3.

24

---

gle. One line, one square, one circle, and one triangle.

Listen and Draw

Here are the chalkboards with the correct shapes drawn on them.

Instructions for This Page

Compare these drawings to those of your children. Point out the similarities and the differences. Be sure to compliment your children on what they drew correctly.

After reviewing your children's drawings, have them look at the sample "answer" drawings in their activity books as the corresponding French words are read again on the tape.

Audio Transcript

Narrator: Here are the same chalkboards, but with my drawings on them. Do your drawings look something like mine? Let's look at each chalkboard together.

Number 1. *Deux lignes et un cercle.*

Number 2. *Deux cercles et une ligne.*

Number 3. *Une ligne, un carré, un cercle, et un triangle.* This is a full chalkboard, isn't it?

1.

Deux lignes et un cercle.

2.

Deux cercles et une ligne.

3.

Une ligne, un carré, un cercle, et un triangle.

25

Look and Say

This activity lets your children verbalize the words they have been hearing on the tape. And since they have to say the French words based solely on looking at the shapes (rather than just reading French words), it also tests their actual knowledge of the words.

Instructions for This Page

Have your children point to the first four shapes and tell you the names of the shapes in French. Next have your children describe what is drawn on each chalkboard.

Encourage your children to use both French shape names and French numbers in describing the contents of the chalkboards.

Have your children pause the tape as needed to have time to give their answers.

 Have your children come up with their own order of shapes and draw them on new "chalkboards." This will encourage them to internalize the language and develop their own creativity.

Audio Transcript

 Narrator: Look at the shapes on your activity book page. As you point to each shape, say what its name is in French.

Number 1. It's *un cercle*. Did you say *un cercle?* That's right.

Number 2. *Un carré.*

Number 3. *Un triangle.*

Number 4. *Une ligne.*

Now chalkboards. Say what you see on each of the chalkboards.

Corresponding Page from Children's Activity Book

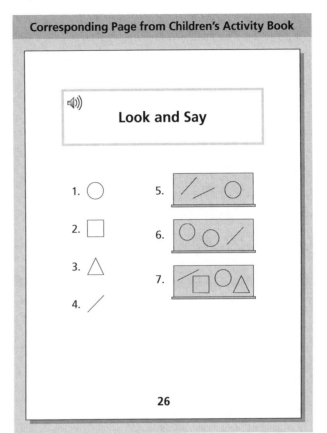

Number 5. *Deux lignes et un cercle.*

Number 6. *Deux cercles et une ligne.*

Number 7. *Une ligne, un carré, un cercle et un triangle.*

Puzzled at the Falls

This section contains an audio transcript of the adventure story your children will hear on the tape.

Instructions for This Page

Have your children listen carefully as the adventure story is read on the tape. Encourage your children to take an active part in listening to the adventure story. Ask them to respond to things they hear and have them say out loud words said by the characters on the tape.

 Younger children might enjoy coloring the picture as the adventure story is read. Older children may want to follow along with the written audio transcript provided in this *Parent's Guide*.

Audio Transcript

 Narrator 2: The Adventure Continues: Puzzled at the Falls

Narrator: After eating breakfast and finishing that activity, you go back to the beach house where you and your cousins are staying and get permission from your aunt and uncle to explore the places shown on the map. You promise to be careful, and then you embark on the first stage of your adventure.

At first your path leads you from the beach up along the bank of a river, and into a high-walled canyon or ravine. The canyon is filled with huge, mossy trees that look very old. Ferns grow around the trunks of the trees, and long, thick vines hang down from the branches to the ground. The calls of jungle birds and other creatures fill the air.

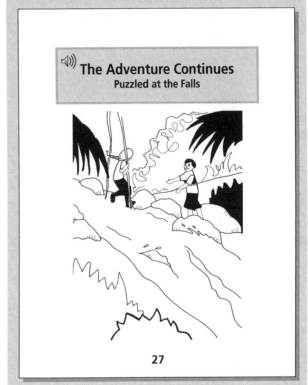

The Adventure Continues
Puzzled at the Falls

27

You don't get too far into the canyon, however, before your path is crossed by the river you have been following. The water is rushing past swiftly, foamy and white over sharp black rocks. You can see the path continue on the other side of the river, but you can see no way to get across.

Jenny: What are we going to do, you guys? Do you think we should try to wade across?

Peter: I don't think so. The water is moving really fast, and those rocks look sharp.

Narrator: "Yeah," you say. "And there's no way to tell how deep it is!"

Jenny: Well how can we find the treasure, then? We have to get across somehow. The map says we need to hike right up this canyon. And you can even see the trail continuing on the other side of the river!

Peter: Wait, you guys, I have an idea! Do you see that vine dangling right down into the river?

Jenny: Yeah...

Continued from Children's Activity Book, page 27

Peter: Well, maybe if we could catch hold of it with a stick or something, we could pull it over to our side of the river, and if it is strong enough, we could swing across the river on it!

Narrator: "Swing on a vine? I think that's just in movies, Peter."

Peter: Well, we could still try it. Look, here's a stick that's long enough... Ugh! It's heavy, though. You hold onto me so I don't slip into the river.... There, I've got hold of the vine.... Well, it feels strong. I'll try first. Whee!!!

Jenny: You made it, Peter! And it looked really fun, too!

Peter: It was! Here, I'll swing the vine back to your side.

Narrator: "Got it!" you say, as you catch the vine in your hand. "Now here I come. Whee!!!"

Peter: Gotcha!

Narrator: Peter catches you and then you swing the vine back to the other side for Jenny to swing across.

Jenny: Here I come! Catch me!... Whee!!! Thanks!

Peter: Are you OK? Alright. Let's get going, you guys. We still have a long way to go to get to the first dot on our map!

Jenny: OK. Let's loop this vine around the tree here, though, so we don't get trapped on this side of the river.

Peter: Good thinking, Jenny. And now, let's go!

Narrator: You hike a bit farther up the valley, pushing your way through jungle ferns and other plants with big green and yellow leaves. At last you come to a waterfall, and the path just seems to stop right in front of it.

Jenny: What does the map say, Peter?

Peter: Well, there is a message here, some kind of riddle, it looks like. But I can't read it. I think some of it's written in French!

Jenny: Well, what does it say?

Peter: It says: "Beyond the *brun et vert,* across the *blanc et noir,* between the *rouge et orange,* and beneath the *jaune et bleu,* you'll find the way ahead." Does that make any sense to you, Jenny?

Jenny: Not really. Those sound like French words, but I don't know what they mean. I think we'd better go back to the beach and ask Derek or Pierre for help.

Peter: OK. I want to swing across the river again anyway!

Narrator: Back at the beach you meet Pierre, who listens to the riddle thoughtfully.

Pierre: I think I know how to help you solve your riddle. And I can actually help you find a part of your treasure at the same time.

Narrator: "Part of our treasure here?" you say. "I don't understand!"

Pierre: Well, come with me into the village. It's not far from where you all are staying. We can all buy sodas at the open air market there, and I'll teach you what you need to know to solve your riddle. Then you can head up the canyon again in the morning. OK?

Peter: Alright, I guess. I want to find the treasure, but we can't do that without solving the riddle anyway. Besides, the village market sounds cool!

Jenny: Yeah, I've never been to an open air market before. It sounds lots more fun than just the grocery store back home.

Narrator: So you, Jenny and Peter walk to the village with Pierre. When you get to the market, Pierre takes you to a soda stand and you each choose your favorite flavor of soda. While you sip your sodas, Pierre offers to teach you the French words for the different colors.

Colors at the Market

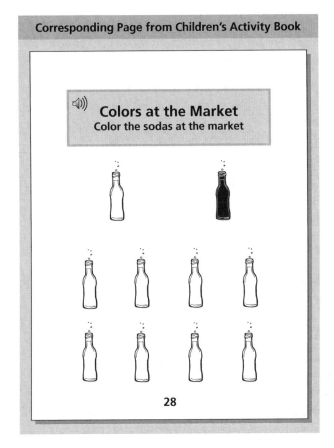

This activity introduces the French words for basic colors: white, black, red, green, yellow, blue, orange, brown, purple and pink.

In this activity, your children are asked to color soda bottles in the different colors in order to help them connect the French words with the various colors. Once the bottles are colored, your children are asked to point to the colors (in French) which they hear on the tape. This reinforces the French color names in their minds.

Instructions for This Page

Have your children use crayons, markers or colored pencils to color in the bottles as the tape directs them. The two bottles in the top row are already colored white and black. Once the bottles are all colored, have your children point to each colored bottle as the tape directs them.

 Since color words in the second half of the activity are reviewed by color rather than by bottle order or number, the order in which your children color the bottles is not important. Simply help them point to the correct colored bottles as the French color words are read. The tape will help them check themselves as well. As ever, try to help your children guess boldly and not worry if they are occasionally wrong.

Audio Transcript

Narrator 2: Activity: Colors at the Market.

Narrator: The bottles on your activity book page are like the ones you see at the market, only the ones on your page aren't colored yet.

To make your bottles look like the ones you see at the market, take out some crayons or markers or colored pencils. You will need these colors, these

couleurs: red, green, yellow, blue, orange, black, brown, purple, pink, and white. A box of sixteen crayons or markers should have all of those. You may stop the tape if you need to go get some.

Have you got something now to color with? Good! Let's begin. As I say the English and French words for a color, pick any one of the empty white bottles on your activity book page and color it in with that color. Stop the tape as often as you need to in order to have time to color. Are you ready? OK. Here we go.

The first soda Pierre points to is a strawberry flavor. It is bright red! So, pick one of the bottles on your page, and color it bright red! Are you finished? Good! The French word for red is *rouge*. That's easy to remember, isn't it? Say it out loud: *rouge*.

The next bottle is a bottle of milk. It is all white. Color one of your bottles white. Pierre points to a bottle of milk and says: *blanc*. Say it out loud: *blanc*. That means "white" in French.

The next bottle Pierre points to has black cherry flavored soda in it. It is black. Color one of your

Continued from Children's Activity Book, page 28

bottles black. The French word for "black" is *noir*. Say it out loud: *noir*.

The next flavor of soda Pierre points to is lime. It is a delicious looking green color. Pick one of your bottles, and color it green. Are you finished? Good! The French word for green is *vert*. Can you remember that? Say it out loud: *vert*.

After that, Pierre points to a lemon flavored soda. It is colored yellow, *jaune*. Say it out loud: *jaune*. Now color one of your bottles *jaune*. Are you finished coloring one of the bottles yellow? Good.

Next Pierre points to a blue colored soda. It is some kind of fruit punch. He tells you that the French word for blue is *bleu*. Say it out loud: *bleu*. So, pick another bottle and color it *bleu*—color it blue. Are you finished? Good.

The next bottle Pierre points to has orange flavor soda in it. Can you guess what color it is? That's right! It is orange! That was too easy! The French word for orange is *orange*. That one is really easy, isn't it! Pick another empty bottle and color it *orange*. Are you finished? Good.

After showing you the orange soda, Pierre points to a cola drink. It is brown. Pick one of your bottles and color it brown. Are you finished? Good! The French word for brown is *brun*. Can you say that? *Brun. Brun.*

The second to last soda Pierre points to is grape flavored—purple. He tells you the French word for purple is *violet*. So, pick one of the bottles you haven't colored yet, and color it *violet*—purple. Are you finished? Good.

The last soda bottle is full of pink lemonade. Pierre points to it and says: *rose. Rose* means pink! That one is easy to remember because it sounds like a rose, and lots of roses are pink. So, color the last bottle *rose*. Are you finished? Excellent!

Well, you should have all the bottles colored in now. That's a lot of colors to learn, isn't it? You aren't sure you'll ever be able to remember them, but Pierre helps you. He says the French words for the colors and lets you point to the soda you think it is. Let's do the same thing together. I'll say a color in French, and you try to point to the right colored soda bottle on your activity book page. Ready? OK, here goes.

Vert. Point to the soda you colored *vert*. Did you point to the green soda? Good! Now another.

Bleu. Point to the soda you colored *bleu*. Did you point to the blue soda? Good. Now another.

Jaune. Point to the soda you colored *jaune*. Did you point to the yellow soda? That's right. Now another.

Rouge. Point to the soda you colored *rouge*. Did you point to the red soda? Well done. Now another.

Rose. Point to the soda you colored *rose*. Did you point to the pink soda? Good. Now another.

Brun. Point to the soda you colored *brun*. Did you point to the brown soda? Right again. Now another.

Orange. Point to the soda you colored *orange*. Did you point to the orange soda? Good. Now one more.

Violet. Point to the soda you colored *violet*. Did you point to the purple soda? Well done.

Scatter Chart

This activity continues to teach French colors by having your children identify and color fruits, vegetables and other things at the market that are the different colors they have learned.

Instructions for This Page

As colors are said on the tape, have your children use crayons, markers or colored pencils to color in the appropriate item.

Audio Transcript

Narrator: Once he has taught you the colors at the soda stand, Pierre takes you around the market, telling you colors and asking you to find things that are those colors. For example, he starts by asking you to find something that is *blanc*, something that is white. You only have to look for a minute to find a man selling milk. Milk is *blanc!*

So let's practice. As I say a color in French, find one of the pictures on your activity book page that is of something which is usually that color. Are you ready? OK. Find something on this page that is usually *jaune*. Did you pick the banana? Good! Bananas are usually *jaune*, aren't they? Go ahead and color the banana *jaune*—yellow. Are you finished coloring the banana *jaune?* Good. Now let's try another color.

Try to find something on this page that is usually *vert*. Can you see anything that is usually *vert*? I see something—the lettuce! Lettuce is usually *vert*, isn't it? So, go ahead and color the lettuce *vert*—green. Are you finished coloring? Good.

Now look at your page and see if there is anything on it that is usually *rouge*. What do you think? Is it the cherries? I'd say so! Cherries are usually very

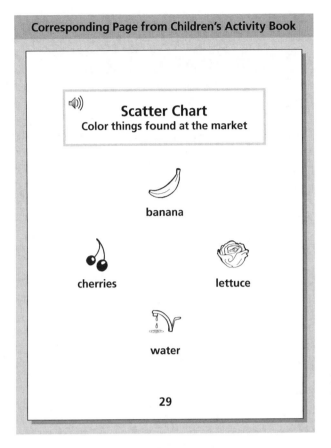

Corresponding Page from Children's Activity Book

Scatter Chart
Color things found at the market

banana

cherries   lettuce

water

29

rouge. So, go ahead and color the cherries *rouge*. Are they colored *rouge* now? Good job.

The last thing on your page is some water. Can you guess what color water is, like in the ocean, or in a lake? That's right! It's blue—*bleu*! So, color the water *bleu*—color it blue. Are you finished? Good.

Match and Learn

This activity tests your children on the four colors reviewed in the previous activity. Your children are asked to point to the correct items based solely on their color names in French.

Instructions for This Page

Have your children point to the items in the various frames that are the colors said on the tape. For instance, when the tape says to point to the item in frame 1 that is *jaune*—yellow, your children should point to the box in that frame which is yellow—the banana.

Have your children pause the tape as needed to have time to give their answers.

Audio Transcript

Narrator: Now that you've learned a few of the French words for colors, let's see which ones you can remember. As I say a color in French, point to the thing in your activity book which is that color. For example, when I say point to something that is *vert*, you point to the lettuce, because it is green. Are you ready? OK, here goes.

Look at the large frame on your activity book page. Point to the thing that is *rouge*. Did you point to the cherries? Good! That's right! A cherry is *rouge*—it is red! Now point to the thing that is *jaune*. Did you point to the banana? Well done! The banana is *jaune*—yellow. Now point to the thing that is *bleu*. Did you choose the water? Good! The water is blue—*bleu!*

Now look at the numbered shapes at the bottom of your page. As I say what each thing is, say out loud what color it is in French!

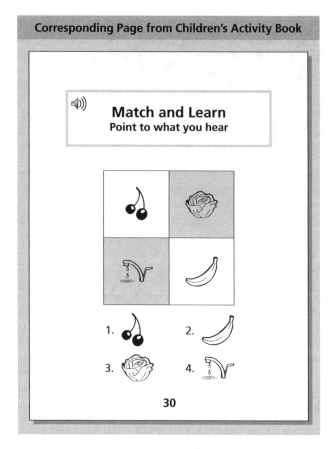

Here we go:

Number 1: A couple of cherries. Did you say *rouge*? That's right! Cherries are *rouge*!

Number 2: A banana. Did you say *jaune*? Yes, bananas are *jaune*.

Number 3: A head of lettuce. Did you say *vert*? Good.

Number 4: Water. Did you say *bleu*? Good.

Scatter Chart

This activity continues to teach French colors by having your children identify and color fruits, vegetables and other things at the market that are the different colors they have learned.

Instructions for This Page

As a color is said on the tape, have your children use crayons, markers or colored pencils to color in the appropriate item.

Audio Transcript

 Narrator: You did a great job remembering those colors. Now let's try to find things that are some other colors.

The next color Pierre asks you to find is *violet*. Can you see something on your page that is often *violet*—often purple? The grapes? Right! You look around the market and find some purple grapes. There are other grapes that are *vert*, but the ones you pick are *violet*. So, take out your colors, and make the grapes purple! Are you finished? Good!

The next color Pierre asks you to find is *brun*—something that is *brun* color. See if you can find something on your page that is usually *brun*. Did you pick the potato? Nice work! Potatoes are usually *brun* color, aren't they? They are usually brown. So, color the potato on your page *brun*.

Next, Pierre asks you to look for something *orange*. See if you can find something on your page that is usually *orange*. Is a carrot usually *orange*? Yes, a carrot usually is *orange*—it usually is orange! So, color the carrot on your page *orange*.

The last thing on your page is a rose. Do you remember the French word for pink? That's right! It's *rose*. Pierre asks you to find something at the market that is *rose*, and you find a beautiful rose. It

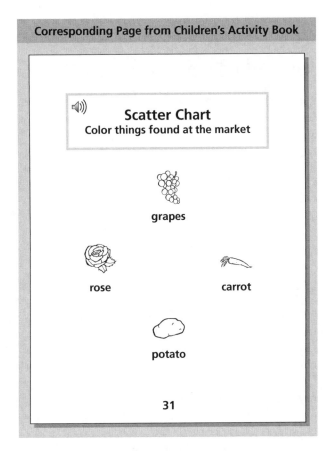

Scatter Chart
Color things found at the market

grapes

rose

carrot

potato

31

is the pinkest thing you've ever seen! So, color the rose on your page *rose*.

Match and Learn

This activity tests your children on the four colors reviewed in the previous activity. Your children are asked to point to the correct items based solely on their color names in French.

Instructions for This Page

Have your children point to the items in the various frames that are the colors said on the tape. For instance, when the tape says to point to the item in frame 1 that is *brun*—brown, your children should point to the box in that frame which is brown—the potato.

Have your children pause the tape as needed to have time to give their answers.

Audio Transcript

Narrator: Now that you've learned a few more of the French words for colors, let's see which ones you can remember. As I say a color in French, point to the thing in your activity book which is that color. For example, when I say point to something that is *brun*, you would point to the potato, because it is brown—*brun*. Are you ready? OK, here goes.

Look at the large frame on your activity book page. Point to the thing that is *violet*. Did you point to the grapes? Good! That's right! Grapes are *violet* in color—they are purple! Now point to the thing that is *orange*. Did you point to the carrot? Well done! Carrots are *orange* color, aren't they? Now point to the thing that is *rose*. Did you choose the rose? Good! The rose is pink, *rose*!

Now look at the numbered shapes at the bottom of your page. As I say what each thing is, say out loud what color it is in French!

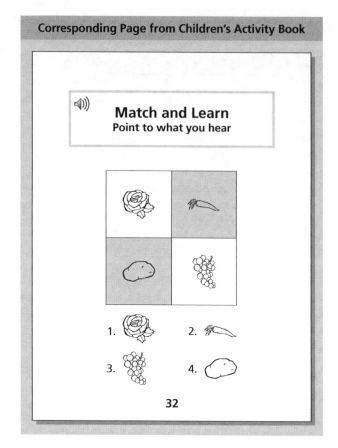

Here we go:

Number 1: A rose. Did you say *rose*? That's right! A rose is *rose*—it is pink.

Number 2: A carrot. Did you say *orange*? That's right! A carrot is *orange*.

Number 3: A bunch of grapes. Did you say *violet*? Good!

Number 4: A potato. Did you say *brun*? Good!

Match and Learn

This activity tests your children on all of the colors learned in this activity. Your children are asked to point to the correct items based solely on their color names in French.

Instructions for This Page

Have your children point to the items in the various frames that are the colors said on the tape.

Audio Transcript

Narrator: Now that we've reviewed the French words for all the colors, let's see which ones you can remember. As I say a color in French, point to the thing in your activity book which is that color. For this exercise, you will also need to remember the French words for black and white. The French word for "black," if you remember, is *noir*. The French word for "white" is *blanc*. *Noir* and *blanc*. Black and white. Now are you ready to review all the colors? Good! As I say the colors, point to the right item in each frame.

Look at frame 1. Point to the thing that is *violet*. Did you point to the grapes? Well done! Now point to the thing that is *blanc*. Did you point to the white bottle? Good job! Now point to the thing that is *jaune*. Did you choose the banana? Nice work. The last thing in this frame is a potato. Do you remember what color a potato is? That's right! It's *brun*—brown.

Now look at frame 2. Can you see something here that is *rouge*? The cherries? Right! How about *orange*? Can you see anything here that is *orange*? The carrot? Correct! And finally, do you see anything *rose* here? The rose? Exactly. The rose is *rose*. Good memory!

Corresponding Page from Children's Activity Book

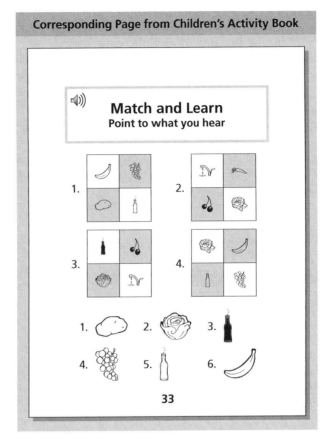

Now look at frame 3. Which of these things is *bleu*? Is it the lettuce? No, the lettuce is *vert*! The water is *bleu*! Now, which thing is *rouge*? The cherries? Right on! And which thing is *noir*? The bottle? That's right! And finally, which thing is *vert*? The lettuce? Of course! We just told you that! And you remembered anyway.

Now look at frame 4. Point to the thing that is *blanc*. Did you point to the white bottle? Well done! Now, point to the thing that is *jaune*. Did you choose the banana? Well done! And now, point to the thing that is *violet*. The grapes, right? You've learned these colors very well.

Now look at the numbered shapes at the bottom of your page. As I say what each thing is, say out loud what color it is in French!

Here we go:

Number 1: A potato. Did you say *brun*? That's right! A potato is *brun*—it is brown.

Number 2: A head of lettuce. Did you say *vert*? That's right!

Continued from Children's Activity Book, page 33

Number 3: A bottle of black cherry soda. Did you say *noir*? Excellent!

Number 4: A bunch of grapes. Did you say *violet*? Good!

Number 5: A bottle of milk. Did you say *blanc*? Well done!

Number 6: A banana. Did you say *jaune*? Perfect!

You've learned your colors very well.

A Snack with Pierre

This section contains an audio transcript of the adventure story your children will hear on the tape.

Instructions for This Page

Have your children listen carefully as the adventure story is read on the tape. Encourage your children to take an active part in listening to the adventure story. Ask them to respond to things they hear and have them say out loud words said by the characters on the tape.

 Younger children might enjoy coloring the picture as the adventure story is read. Older children may want to follow along with the written audio transcript provided in this *Parent's Guide*.

When your children get to the part of the adventure story where Pierre makes french fries, stop the tape and turn to the Recipes section at the back of this *Parent's Guide* to find the recipe. Try making some!

Audio Transcript

 Narrator 2: The Adventure Continues: A Snack with Pierre

Peter: It sure was fun to learn the French colors that way.

Pierre: I'm glad you enjoyed it, Peter! And that's the piece of the treasure I promised you: Make learning fun. If you learn by doing something fun, you'll remember things better and you want to learn more!

Peter: Make learning fun. That's a strange clue in a treasure hunt, but we'll remember it.

Jenny: Yeah.

Corresponding Page from Children's Activity Book

Narrator: "Well, it's almost night time now," you say. "I guess we'd better wait until tomorrow to hike back up in the canyon to the waterfall. I can hardly wait to solve the riddle though! I hope morning comes fast!"

Peter: Yeah, me too.

Pierre: I bet that it won't if you're that excited! But I have an idea. How about you all come back to our house with me before dinner, and I'll tell you a story like the one Derek told you this morning, using French. I think you'll want to have heard this story when you get to the waterfall again tomorrow. There's a moral to it that will help you.

Jenny: That sounds great, Pierre. We need all the help we can get on this adventure. And it's fun to hear stories told in French, too.

Narrator: "Yeah," you agree. "And we always learn lots of new words, too."

Pierre: Exactly. Well, let's go then.

Continued from Children's Activity Book, page 35

Narrator: So you all walk back down the path to Derek's house on the beach. For a snack, Pierre has you help him slice potatoes into strips to make *frites*, French fries. Then, out in front of the house, you stretch out comfortably in hammocks and Pierre begins his story, a story about a boy who one day met a fierce bear!

A Boy and a Bear

Although it is important for children to first understand language, it is exciting when they begin to use it, and that is where the learning really takes off. This activity moves in that direction. It is very close in format to the earlier, "A Girl and a Rat" activity.

Instructions for This Page

Have your children look at the first page of the story "A Boy and a Bear" and listen to the introduction to the story on the tape.

Audio Transcript

Narrator 2: Activity: A Boy and a Bear.

Narrator: Here is the story Pierre tells you. It is called *Un Garçon et un Ours:* A Boy and a Bear.

Corresponding Page from Children's Activity Book

A Boy and a Bear
Une Histoire

36

Match and Learn

This activity is visual, audio, and kinesthetic. It is designed to help your children learn by listening and pointing.

Instructions for This Page

Have your children point to the correct boxes and pictures as the tape instructs. In the second part of the activity, have them answer out loud the questions asked about the numbered pictures.

Have your children pause the tape as needed to have time to give their answers.

Audio Transcript

Narrator: You already know some of these words. Let's go over them. First, point to *le rat*. Did you point to the rat, in the top white box? Good. Now, point to *le garçon,* the boy. *Le garçon* is in the top gray box, right? Next, point to the bear, *l'ours. L'ours* is in the top white box, right? No, *l'ours* is in the bottom gray box. Now, point to the *fille*, the girl. The *fille* is in the bottom white box, right? Good.

Now, see if you can answer some questions about the words you just learned. Look at the picture with the number one next to it.

Number 1. Is this a *garçon* or a *rat*? A *rat*? No, this is a *garçon,* a boy.

Number 2. Is this an *ours*? Yes, it is an *ours*, it is a bear.

Number 3. This is a *fille,* right? No, this is a *rat.*

Number 4. This one's an *ours*, right? No, this one is a *fille.*

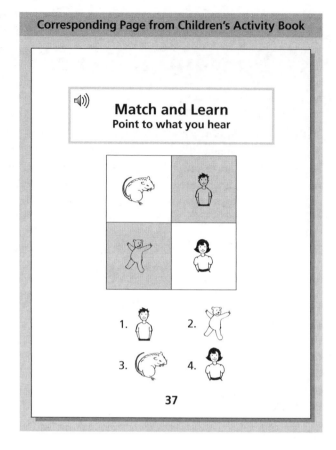

Corresponding Page from Children's Activity Book

Match and Learn
Point to what you hear

1.   2.
3.   4.

37

Diglot Weave

This activity begins a simple bilingual or diglot weave narrative built around two of the characters from the previous activities. This type of narrative was originally introduced as a language learning aid by Professor Rudy Lentulay of Bryn Mawr University.

Instructions for This Page

Have your children listen carefully and follow the story in their activity books as it is told on the tape.

 Have your children follow the words and pictures of the story with their finger, so that when the tape says the French word for "bear," for instance, their finger is pointing to the picture of the bear. This kinesthetic connection will enhance their mental connections between the French words and the ideas they represent.

Audio Transcript

 Narrator: Now listen to Pierre's story about a boy, a *garçon*, and a bear, an *ours*. Follow along and look at the pictures.

Un garçon sees *un ours. L'ours* sees *le garçon. L'ours* roars--rrr! *Le garçon* roars--rrr! *L'ours* goes toward *le garçon*, roaring--rrr! *Le garçon* goes toward *l'ours*, roaring--rrr! *L'ours* hesitates, then turns back and runs. *Le garçon* doesn't hesitate. *Le garçon* chases *l'ours*. But *l'ours* escapes. *Le garçon* sits down *et rit. L'ours* sits down *et pleure*.

Were you able to follow along? Good.

Corresponding Page from Children's Activity Book

Diglot Weave
Un Garçon et un Ours

👤 sees 🧸 . 🧸 sees 👤

🧸 roars—rrr!

👤 roars—rrr!

🧸 goes toward 👤 , roaring—rrr!

👤 goes toward 🧸 , roaring—rrr!

🧸 hesitates, then turns back, and runs.

👤 doesn't hesitate.

👤 chases 🧸 . But 🧸 escapes.

👤 🪑 and 😃 .

🧸 🪑 and 😢 .

38

Match and Learn

This activity uses frames once again to introduce some new pictures that can then be incorporated into the telling of the story.

Instructions for This Page

Have your children point to the correct pictures as the tape instructs.

Audio Transcript

Narrator: Before I tell this story again, I'll teach you some more words in French.

Look at frame 1. Point to the box with the boy and the roar sound. This is the top gray box. These two pictures together mean "boy roars." In French "bear roars" is *ours grogne*. Now, point to *garçon voit ours*, "boy sees bear." *Garçon voit ours* is in the top white box, right? Now point to *ours voit garçon*, "bear sees boy." Did you point to the bottom gray box? Good. Let's keep going.

Look at frame 2. Point to "boy goes toward." This is in the top white box. Do you see it? The big arrow next to the boy means "goes toward." In French it's *avance vers,* goes toward. So the picture in the top white box means *garçon avance vers,* "boy goes toward." Now point to *ours avance vers*. It's in the top, gray box, right? Good job. Now point to *garçon poursuit ours.* It is in the bottom gray box, right? Good. Do you remember what *poursuit* means? It means chases? That's right. Now point to "bear hesitates, then turns back." This picture is in the bottom white box. In French it is, *ours hésite, se retire.*

Now look at frame 3. Point to "boy sits." The arrow pointing to the chair means "sits." In French "boy sits" is *garçon s'assied*. So, point to *garçon s'assied*. It's in the bottom gray box, right? Good job. Now point to *ours s'assied*. It's in the top gray

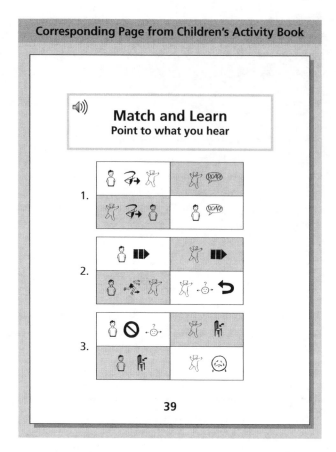

box, right? Now point to "the boy does not hesitate," *garçon n'hésite pas*. It's in the top white box, right?

Match and Learn

This activity uses frames once again to introduce a couple more new pictures that can then be incorporated into the telling of the story.

Instructions for This Page

Have your children point to the pictures as directed by the tape.

Have your children pause the tape as needed to have time to give their answers.

Audio Transcript

 Narrator: You're doing fine with these new French words. Let's learn some more.

Look at frame 4. Do you remember what "hesitates" is in French? That's right, it's *hésite*. Point to *ours hésite*. It's in the bottom gray box, right? Now point to *garçon avance vers ours*. It's is in the top white box, right? Good. Now point to *garçon n'hésite pas*. Did you point to the top gray box? Good. Now point to *ours s'assied*. It's in the bottom white box, right?

Now look at frame 5. Point to *ours pleure*. Did you point to the top gray box? That's right. Now point to *ours hésite, se retire, court*. Can you guess which one that is? Did you choose the top white box? Right again! Now point to *garçon s'assied*. It's is in the bottom gray box, right? Good. Now point to *garçon rit*. Did you point to the bottom white box? Good.

Now look at frame 6. Point to *garçon n'hésite pas*. Did you point to the bottom white box? Good. Now point to *ours s'échappe*. "Bear escapes" is in the bottom gray box. right? Now point to *ours s'assied et pleure*. It is in the top white box, right? Now point to *garçon poursuit ours*. Did you point to the top gray box? Very well done!

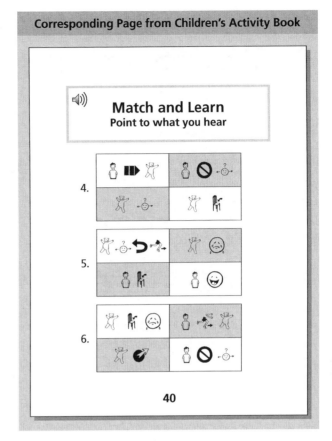

Rebus Story

This activity is designed to help your children begin to think in French. This is accomplished by having pictures in the activity book represent the French words read on the tape. This way the children will associate the French words with their English equivalents. The French words and ideas will be directly associated in their minds.

Instructions for This Page

Have your children follow the pictures with their finger as the French words for those pictures are read on the tape.

 This is a good activity for drawing pictures and creating flashcards.
Encourage your children to create stories of their own!

Audio Transcript

 Narrator: Now that you know the story, try to follow the pictures as I tell you the story all in French. Are you ready? Here we go!

Un garçon voit un ours. L'ours voit le garçon. L'ours grogne--rrr! Le garçon grogne--rrr! L'ours avance vers garçon, grogne--rrr! Le garçon avance vers ours, grogne--rrr! L'ours hésite, se retire, court. Le garçon n'hésite pas. Le garçon poursuit l'ours. Mais l'ours s'échappe. Le garçon s'assied et rit. L'ours s'assied et pleure.

Were you able to understand the entire story? Very good.

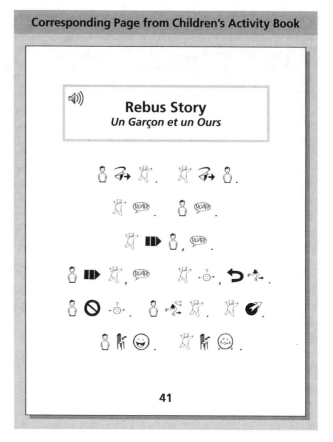

Describe What You See

This activity requires your children to use the French words they learned in the previous activity to describe the pictures they see.

Instructions for This Page

Have your children say the French words for the pictures, or write them on the blank lines to the side of the pictures.

Have your children say or write in as many of the French words as they can on their own. Then you may go back through with them and help them remember those they missed. Continue to encourage them to guess when they need to, and to not feel bad when they cannot remember all the words or when they get one wrong.

Audio Transcript

Narrator: On this page are some of the pictures you have learned the words for. Say the French words for the pictures. Or if you like, write the French words for the pictures in the blanks.

Corresponding Page from Children's Activity Book

Story Telling

This activity lets your children use the French words they have learned to tell the story of "A Boy and a Bear" themselves.

Instructions for This Page

Have your children follow the trail of pictures (from top to bottom) with their finger, telling the story using the French words for the pictured items as they go.

 If your children cannot remember a particular word let them think for a moment, and then go ahead and help them. Your goal here is to encourage them to think as hard as they can on their own, while keeping them from getting frustrated or discouraged. Encourage them to create their own stories using the pictures in this activity.

Audio Transcript

 Narrator: Follow the trail of pictures from top to bottom with your finger, telling the story using the French words for the pictures.

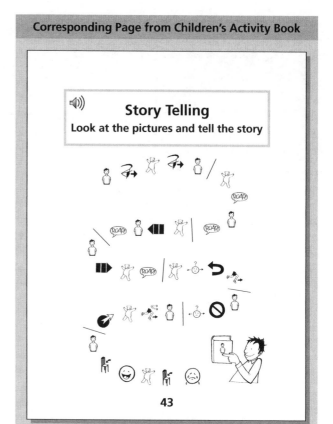

Practice in French

This activity asks your children to tell the story on their own, using the French words they have learned, and using the pictures in the circle as memory prompts.

Instructions for This Page

Have your children look at the pictures in the circle and try to tell the story on their own, using the French words they have leaned. Have them record how long it takes them to tell the complete story in French their first time, and then their best subsequent time.

 Let your children try telling the story as many as six or eight times, each time trying to improve their speed.

Audio Transcript

 Narrator: Last of all, use the pictures in the big circle on your activity book page to tell the story again, using the French words you have learned. Point to the pictures as you go along, and write down in the first box how long it takes you to tell the story the first time. Then tell the story a few more times, and write down your fastest time in the second box. I'll tell you the story now one more time in French, to help you remember all the words.

Un garçon voit un ours. L'ours voit le garçon. L'ours grogne--rrr! Le garçon grogne--rrr! L'ours avance vers garçon, grogne--rrr! Le garçon avance vers ours, grogne--rrr! L'ours hésite, se retire, court. Le garçon n'hésite pas. Le garçon poursuit l'ours. Mais l'ours s'échappe. Le garçon s'assied et rit. L'ours s'assied et pleure.

Now you tell the story and record your times.

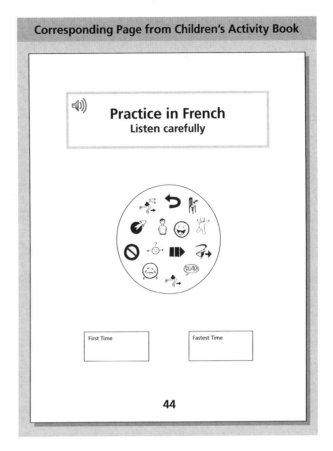

Were you able to tell the story on your own? Good. What was your fastest time?

Bananas Anyone?

This section contains an audio transcript of the adventure story your children will hear on the tape.

Instructions for This Page

Have your children listen carefully as the adventure story is read on the tape. Encourage your children to take an active part in listening to the adventure story. Ask them to respond to things they hear and have them say out loud words said by the characters on the tape.

 Younger children might enjoy coloring the picture as the adventure story is read. Older children may want to follow along with the written audio transcript provided in this *Parent's Guide.*

Audio Transcript

 Narrator 2: The Adventure Continues: Bananas, Anyone?

Jenny: That was a good story, Pierre. I liked it, and I loved those homemade French fries!

Peter: Yeah, me too. Now we just need to figure out what the moral of the story is so we can use it when we get to the waterfall tomorrow. I wonder what the moral is?

Narrator: "I'm not sure I know what it is either," you say. "But I guess maybe we'll have to wait to guess until we solve the riddle."

Pierre: That's right. Good luck!

Narrator: With that you, Jenny and Peter head back to your beach house for a restless night's sleep. Early the next morning you set out for the jungle canyon once more. As you hike along the beach and then up into the trees, the sun is just

---

Corresponding Page from Children's Activity Book

🔊 **The Adventure Continues**
Bananas Anyone?

45

---

beginning to peek over the hills at the middle of the island. It's chilly and damp in the canyon, and you are careful not to let your feet get wet as you swing over the river. Once you are across you hurry to the end of the trail and take out our map. The riddle reads: "Beyond the *brun et vert,* across the *blanc et noir,* between the *rouge et orange,* and beneath the *jaune et bleu,* you'll find the way ahead."

Peter: Now it makes sense!

Jenny: Yeah. It means, "Beyond the brown and green, across the black and white, between the red and orange, and beneath the yellow and blue is the way ahead." So, what are the colors all about?

Narrator: "I think I get it," you say. "The colors are for things in this canyon. Like the brown and green, for example. The tree trunks are brown, and the leaves are green. And the water rushing in the river is white, and the rocks are black."

Jenny: Oh, yeah, I get it now too. There are red flowers on that side of this waterfall, and oranges

Continued from Children's Activity Book, page 45

growing on the tree on this side! And the sky is blue and the sun is yellow. So the place we have to find is beyond the trees and across the river, and between the flowers and the tree, and under the sun and the sky!

Peter: But how could that be right? We have gone past the trees and across the river, but between the flowers and the orange tree and under the sun and the sky is the waterfall! How can we find a way ahead in the waterfall?

Jenny: I don't know. But isn't that what the map says?

Peter: I think so. But I still don't know what to do. It looks like we'll just have to go back again and ask Derek or Pierre for help.

Narrator: "Wait," you say. "I have another idea. Remember how Pierre told us that we'd need to figure out what the moral of the 'Boy and the Bear' story was, and use it here?"

Peter: Yeah, but what does that mean we should do?

Narrator: "Well," you reply, "what did the boy in the story do when the bear roared at him?"

Jenny: He was really brave and he just roared back, and then the bear ran away.

Narrator: "Right," you say. "He was really daring. So maybe that's what we need to do: just be really daring."

Peter: I think I get what you're saying. So if we're like the boy in the story, instead of backing down from this waterfall, we should be daring and do what the riddle says: look for the way ahead through the waterfall!

Narrator: "Right!" you reply. "I guess. Now we just have to figure out how to do that."

Jenny: Well, I'm ready to get wet, I guess. It's a really hot day anyway. I'll try reaching my arm through the water first.

Narrator: So Jenny reaches her arm through the water, but she can't feel anything. So then you try,

and then Peter too. "It seems like it's hollow behind the falls!" you exclaim.

Peter: Yeah! I'll bet that's the secret! There must be a hollowed out place behind the waterfall, hidden by the water!

Jenny: I bet you're right, Peter. I'm gonna try it.

Narrator: With that, Jenny steps boldly right through the waterfall, holding out her arms in front of her so she won't run into anything. As she passes through the falls she shivers out loud at the cold water, and then she disappears.

Peter: Hey, Jenny, are you all right?

Jenny: Yeah! It is hollow back here, you guys. And there's a ladder here that goes up to the top of the cliff. Come on in, there's just enough room for all of us!

Narrator: "I'm coming," you call back, and then you too duck under the water and come out next to Jenny in the dry hollow spot on the other side. A moment later Peter jumps through the sheet of water too, and you all stand wet but excited in the hollow of the rock.

Jenny: Wow, you guys, this is cool. From outside we couldn't see this ladder at all!

Peter: Yeah. It was hidden by the waterfall and the tree. But I bet if we duck our heads we can climb up it without getting wet again. Let's try!

Jenny: Alright!

Narrator: "We made it," you say, as you finish climbing the ladder and step out on top of the cliff. "Wow, it doesn't look so far down from here. The cliffs seemed lots bigger when we were looking up."

Peter: I think so too. And hey, look at the ocean! From up here you can see it stretching out for miles!

Jenny: Yeah. It's so blue.

Narrator: The view from on top of the cliff really is breathtaking. You all stare out to sea for a few minutes, then, remembering your map and the

Continued from Children's Activity Book, page 45

path leading inland, you turn and look toward the middle of the island. "Hey," you say, "look at those trees up ahead, they look like banana trees!"

Peter: Yeah, and the first dot on the map seems to be right in the middle of them. Let's go!

Narrator: So you follow the path marked on your map right into the middle of a whole forest of banana trees, all with big bunches of bananas hanging from their branches. As you hike on through the trees, you hear the sound of chopping, and a minute later you walk into a clearing where a man is standing with a big bunch of bananas in one hand, and a machete in the other. It looks like he has just cut the bunch of bananas from one of the trees, and with the machete in his hand, he looks a bit dangerous at first.

Phillip: *Bonjour!*

Narrator: *"Bonjour!"* you say.

Phillip: *Je suis* Phillip. *Qui sont vous?*

Peter: *Je suis* Peter.

Jenny: *Et je suis* Jenny.

Narrator: You introduce yourself in French as well, and then Phillip says:

Phillip: *Oui.* I've been expecting you! My friend Derek, the fisherman, passed this way earlier this morning and told me you might be coming by, once you solved the riddle of the waterfall. I have the next part of your treasure, but to get it you'll have to eat this entire bunch of bananas all by yourselves!

Jenny: But... it's huge!

Peter: Yeah. There must be fifty bananas on there. We can't eat all those! It's impossible! It would take a giant to eat all those bananas at once.

Narrator: "Yeah. It's not fair," you agree.

Phillip: (laughing heartily) Ha, ha, ha! You're right. It is impossible. And it's not fair. And... I'm only joking. Actually, I'm just getting around to giving you the next part of your treasure. It is this: DON'T

STRESS! If you're ever going to learn anything like a new language, the easiest way to do it is to just don't stress. Don't get worried about how fast you're progressing or how many new words you've learned. Just pick up whatever you can, whenever and where ever you can. Trying to learn a whole language in a day would, after all, be like trying to eat all these bananas at once!

Peter: I understand. OK. Don't stress is the next clue. That makes three: Build on what you know, Make learning fun, and Don't stress.

Phillip: Good memory, Peter. Now, if you three would be willing to help me work my plantation for a couple of hours, I'll tell you a story about someone who could eat all these bananas at once!

Jenny: Really?

Phillip: Yes. It's about a giant, just as Peter said. Here, here's a cutlass for each of you.

Peter: A cutlass? Is that another word for machete?

Phillip: Yes. But we call them cutlasses here.

Peter: That's cool. It sounds like pirate stuff.

Phillip: I guess it does. But you'll just use these to chop down the old banana trees that aren't good anymore, OK?

Narrator: "Alright," you say. "We'll do our best."

Phillip: Excellent. And I'll tell you the story about the giant while we work.

Peter: OK. But, Phillip, before you tell the story, I have a question.

Phillip: Yes?

Peter: I was wondering... when you speak French it sounds different than Derek or Pierre. It sounds like you speak with a different accent.

Phillip: That's true, Peter. I do. That's because Derek is originally from Tahiti, a French speaking island near Australia and New Zealand.

Jenny: Tahiti. That sounds like a really interesting place, we'll have to ask Derek about it! But do they

Continued from Children's Activity Book, page 45

speak French there too? I thought people only spoke French in France, and on a few islands like this.

Phillip: Actually, Jenny, people speak French in lots of places besides France. Why, just in Europe alone there are people who speak French in Switzerland, Luxembourg, and Belgium. And there are also people who speak French in Algeria and Haiti, and in parts of Canada, Senegal and Morocco.

Jenny: Wow. That's a lot of places! But where are you from, then, Phillip?

Phillip: I'm actually from France itself, the birth-place of the French language. You'll find that those of us who are or were originally citizens of France are very proud of our cultural heritage and our nation. We are all great patriots, and we pre-serve our language carefully. Fashion is also very important in France. We like to stay up with the latest trends, and always look and dress our best in public. Good food is also greatly appreciated in France, and we especially enjoy having big lunches. France itself is about the size of the state of Texas, making it the largest country in Western Europe. French people like sports, too—especially individual sports like fishing, tennis, hiking, skiing, sailing and cycling. In fact, the greatest bicycle race in the world, the Tour de France, is held there every year.

Peter: Wow! France sounds like a really exciting place.

Jenny: Yeah. Thanks for telling us about it. I hope we get to visit there someday!

Phillip: You would love it. Now, let me tell you the story of the hungry giant.

A Hungry Giant

It is important for children to first understand spoken language, but it is more exciting when they begin to use it, and that is where the learning really takes off. In this activity we continue with comprehension building, but as the activities progress, we gradually introduce conversation.

Your children will hear a story about a hungry giant several times. They will learn the character names and identify them with pictures. By the time we get to their telling the story, they will have learned to recognize the pictures well enough that they can pretty much tell the story simply by looking at the pictures.

Instructions for This Page

Have your children look at the first page of the story "A Hungry Giant" and listen to the introduction to the story on the tape.

Audio Transcript

Narrator 2: Activity: A Hungry Giant.

Narrator: This is the story of "A Hungry Giant."

Match and Learn

This activity is visual, audio, and kinesthetic. It is designed to help your children learn by listening and pointing.

Instructions for This Page

Have your children point to the correct boxes and pictures as the tape instructs. In the second part of the activity have them answer out loud the questions asked about the numbered pictures. The purpose of this activity is simply to teach the system of frames and numbered pictures in preparation for French learning using these tools in subsequent sections.

Have your children pause the tape as needed to have time to give their answers.

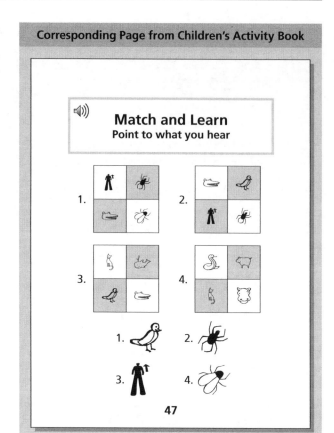

Corresponding Page from Children's Activity Book

Audio Transcript

 Narrator: Before I tell you this *histoire*, I'll teach you some new words to help you understand.

Look at frame 1. Point to the giant, the *géant*. The *géant* is in the top white box, right? Now point to the crocodile, the *crocodile*. The *crocodile* is in the bottom gray box, right? Now point to the fly, the *mouche*. Is the *mouche* in the top gray box? No, the *mouche* is in the bottom white box, right? Now point to the spider, the *araignée*. It is in the top gray box, right?

Now look at frame 2. Point to the *araignée*. It is in the bottom white box, right? Now point to the *crocodile*. He is in the top white box, right? Now point to the *géant*. It is in the bottom gray box, right? Now point to the *oiseau*, the bird. It is in the top gray box, right?

Now look at frame 3. Point to the *oiseau*. It is in the top gray box, right? No, the *oiseau* is in the bottom gray box. Now point to the whale, the *baleine*. It is in the top gray box, right? Now point to the *chat*,

the cat. It is in the top white box, right? Yes. Now point to the *crocodile*. It is in the bottom gray box, right? No, it is in the bottom white box.

Now look at frame 4. Point to the hippopotamus, the *hippopotame*. The *hippopotame* is in the bottom white box, right? Yes. Now point to the *cochon,* the pig. The *cochon* is in the top gray box, right? Now point to the *serpent*, the snake. The *serpent* is in the bottom gray box, right? No, the *serpent* is in the top white box. Now point to the *chat*. The *chat* is in the bottom gray box, right?

Now see if you can answer some questions about the words you just learned. Look at the picture with the number one next to it.

Number 1. Is this a *oiseau?* Yes, this is a *oiseau*.

Number 2. Is this an *araignée?* Yes, this is an *araignée*.

Number 3. Is this a *géant* or a *mouche?* Did you say a giant, a *géant?* Yes, this is a *géant*.

Number 4. Is this an *araignée?* No, this is a *mouche*.

Match and Learn

This activity uses frames once again to introduce some new pictures and words that can then be incorporated into the telling of the story.

Instructions for This Page

Have your children point to the correct pictures as the tape instructs. In the second part of the activity have them answer out loud the questions asked about the numbered pictures.

 As these activities become progressively more challenging, the main objective is to help your children feel confident. They should not be overly concerned with correctness. Encourage them to point boldly as soon as they hear what to point to in the first part of the activity, and to speak out loud in response to the questions in the second half. When your children guess wrong, let them know it's okay and to keep making their best guesses.

Audio Transcript

 Narrator: Did you do well with those pictures and words? Good. Let's try a few more.

Look at frame 5. Point to the *léopard*. The *léopard*, the leopard, is in the top gray box, right? Now point to the *géant*. The *géant* is in the bottom white box, right? No, it is in the bottom gray box. Now point to the *mouche*. The *mouche* is in the bottom white box, right? Yes. Now point to the *crocodile* . It's in the top white box, right? Yes!

Now look at frame 6. Point to the *léopard et* the *mouche*. They are in the top gray box, right? Yes. Now point to the *crocodile et* the *baleine*. They are in the bottom gray box, right? No, they are in the top white box. Point to the *oiseau et* the *crocodile*. The *oiseau et* the *crocodile* are in the bottom gray box,

right? Yes. Now point to the *serpent* and the *cochon*. The *serpent et* the *cochon* are in the bottom white box, right?

Now look at frame 7. Point to the *géant*. The *géant* is in the bottom white box, right? Yes. He is. Now point to the *baleine*. It is in the top gray box, right? Yes. Now point to the *araignée*. Is it in the bottom white box? No, it is in the bottom gray box. Now point to the *crocodile*. It's in the top white box, right? Yes.

Now, see if you can answer some questions about the words you just learned.

Look at picture number 1. Is this a *oiseau?* Yes, this is a *oiseau*.

Picture number 2. Is this a *crocodile* or a *mouche?* It is a *mouche*.

Picture number 3. Is this a *baleine?* No, this is a *hippopotame*.

Picture number 4 is a *crocodile,* right? No, it is a *baleine*.

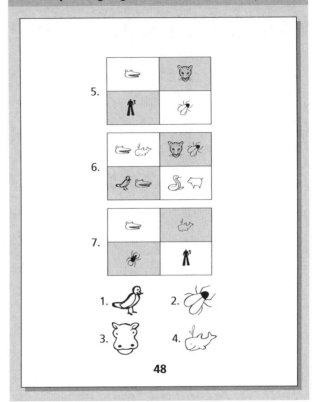

48

Match and Learn

This activity uses frames once again to introduce some new pictures that can then be incorporated into the telling of the story.

Instructions for This Page

Have your children point to the correct pictures as the tape instructs. Have your children pause the tape as needed to have time to give their answers.

 Have your children come up with frames of their own! These can then be used as flashcards.

Audio Transcript

 Narrator: Here are a few more pictures and new words to learn.

Look at frame 1. Point to the *serpent*. It is in the top white box, right? Yes. Now point to the *crocodile a mangé l'araignée*, "the crocodile ate the spider." It is in the bottom gray box, right? Yes. Now point to the *baleine a mangé le crocodile*. Is "the whale ate the crocodile" in the bottom white box? Yes, it is. Now point to the boy likes, *le garçon aime bien*. It's in the top gray box.

Now look at frame 2. Point to *homme a pensé*, "man thought." *Homme a pensé* is in the top white box, right? Yes. Now point to the *chat a pensé*. Can you guess what this means? That's right! It means, "cat thought." It's in the bottom gray box, right? Yes. Now point to the *crocodile a mangé l'oiseau*. That's in the bottom white box, right? Now point to *le garçon n'aime pas*. That is in the bottom gray box, right? No, it is in the top gray box. *Le garçon n'aime pas* means "the boy does not like."

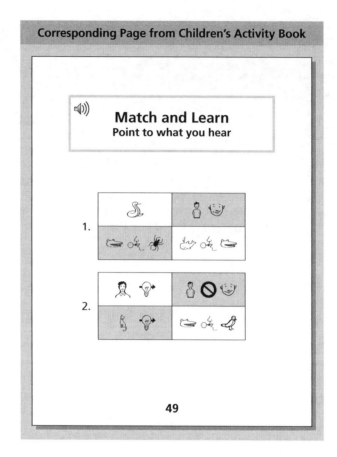

Corresponding Page from Children's Activity Book

🔊 **Match and Learn**
Point to what you hear

1.

2.

49

Describe What You See

This activity requires your children to use the French words they learned in the previous activities to describe the pictures they see.

Instructions for This Page

Have your children say the French words for the pictures, or write them on the blank lines to the side of the pictures.

Have your children say or write in as many of the French words as they can on their own. Then you may go back through with them and help them remember those they missed. Continue to encourage them to guess when they need to, and to not feel bad when they cannot remember all the words or when they get one wrong.

Audio Transcript

Narrator: On this page are some of the pictures you have learned the words for. Say the French words for the pictures. Or if you like, write the French words for the pictures in the blanks.

Diglot Weave

The following multi-page activity contains an extended diglot weave narrative built around the words from the previous activities.

Instructions for This Page

Have your children listen carefully and follow the story in their activity books as it is told on the tape.

 Have your children follow the words and pictures of the story with their finger, so that when the tape says the French word for "giant," for instance, their finger points to the picture of the giant. This kinesthetic connection will enhance their mental connections between the French words and the ideas they represent.

If the pace is ever too fast, stop the tape and review with your children. Be sure to reward understanding and encourage listening. The activity is designed to help your children develop comprehension of main ideas. You may wish to point to the pictures and have them give the French equivalents. Keep in mind, however, that comprehension of every word is not nearly as important as overall comprehension—understanding the main ideas of the story.

Audio Transcript

 Narrator: Now listen to the story of "A Hungry Giant." Follow along and look at the pictures.

Have you ever seen a *géant*? Do you know how big a *géant* is? *Sais-tu* how much a *géant* can eat? I haven't ever seen a *géant*, but one time my father (*mon père*) saw one. Anyway *mon père* told me he saw one. This happened when he was just *un garçon* your age.

 Diglot Weave
A Hungry Giant

Have you ever seen a *géant*? Do you know how big a *géant* is? *Sais-tu* how much a *géant* can eat? I haven't ever seen a *géant*, but one time my father (*mon père*) saw one. Anyway *mon père* told me he saw one. This happened when he was just *un garçon* your age.

51

Diglot Weave

This is the next section of the multi-page diglot weave narrative of "A Hungry Giant."

Instructions for This Page

Have your children continue to listen carefully and follow the story in their activity books as it is told on the tape.

Audio Transcript

Narrator: One morning before breakfast he took a walk and saw *une mouche* that was caught in a spider's web. He watched *l'araignée* come and eat the fly.

Très bien! ("Good!") thought *mon père*. *"L'araignée* ate *la mouche*. I don't like flies…*Je n'aime pas les mouches."*

One morning before breakfast he took a walk and saw *une mouche* that was caught in a spider's web. He watched *l'araignée* come and eat the fly.

Très bien! ("Good!") thought *mon père*. "*L'araignée* ate *la mouche*. I don't like flies . . . *Je n'aime pas les mouches."*

52

Diglot Weave

This is the next section of the multi-page diglot weave narrative of "A Hungry Giant."

Instructions for This Page

Have your children continue to listen carefully and follow the story in their activity books as it is told on the tape.

Audio Transcript

Narrator: A moment later, a *oiseau* came and a *mangé l'araignée.* "*Très bien,*" thought *mon père.* "*L'oiseau* ate *l'araignée. Je n'aime pas les araignées.*"

The next moment *un chat* came along *et a mangé l'oiseau. Et mon père a pensé:* "Too bad (*Dommage*); *j'aime bien les oiseaux.*"

A moment later, a *oiseau* came and a *mangé l'araignée.* "*Très bien,*" thought *mon père.* "*L'oiseau* ate *l'araignée. Je n'aime pas les araignées.*"

The next moment *un chat* came along *et a mangé l'oiseau. Et mon père a pensé:* "Too bad (*Dommage*); *j'aime bien les oiseaux.*"

53

Diglot Weave

This is the next section of the multi-page diglot weave narrative of "A Hungry Giant."

Instructions for This Page

Have your children continue to listen carefully and follow the story in their activity books as it is told on the tape.

Audio Transcript

 Narrator: The next moment *un serpent* came along *et a mangé le chat. Et mon père a pensé:* "*Dommage, j'aime bien les chats.*"

The next moment *un cochon* came along *et a mangé le serpent. Et mon père a pensé:* "*Très bien, le cochon* ate *le serpent. Je n'aime pas les serpents.*"

Corresponding Page from Children's Activity Book

The next moment *un serpent* came along *et a mangé le chat. Et mon père a pensé:* "*Dommage, j'aime bien les chats.*"

The next moment *un cochon* came along *et a mangé le serpent. Et mon père a pensé:* "*Très bien, le cochon* ate *le serpent. Je n'aime pas les serpents.*"

54

Diglot Weave

This is the next section of the multi-page diglot weave narrative of "A Hungry Giant."

Instructions for This Page

Have your children continue to listen carefully and follow the story in their activity books as it is told on the tape.

Audio Transcript

 Narrator: Before long *un léopard* came along *et a mangé le cochon. Et mon père a pensé:* "Wow! *Un léopard* ate *le cochon.* This is exciting!"

A while later *un crocodile* came along *et a mangé le léopard. Et mon père a pensé:* "Wow, *un croco-dile* ate *le léopard.* This is really exciting. What will happen now?"

Corresponding Page from Children's Activity Book

Before long *un léopard* came along *et a mangé le cochon. Et mon père a pensé:* "Wow! *Un léopard* ate *le cochon.* This is exciting!"

A while later *un crocodile* came along *et a mangé le léopard. Et mon père a pensé:* "Wow, *un crocodile* ate *le léopard.* This is really exciting. What will happen now?"

55

Diglot Weave

This is the next section of the multi-page diglot weave narrative of "A Hungry Giant."

Instructions for This Page

Have your children continue to listen carefully and follow the story in their activity books as it is told on the tape.

Audio Transcript

Narrator: Before long *un hippopotame* came along *et a mangé le crocodile. Et mon père a pensé:* "Wow, *un hippopotame* ate *le crocodile.* What will happen now?"

A moment later *une baleine* came along *et a mangé l'hippopotame. Et mon père a pensé:* "Wow, this is too much!

Corresponding Page from Children's Activity Book

Before long *un hippopotame* came along *et a mangé le crocodile. Et mon père a pensé:* "Wow, *un hippopotame* ate *le crocodile.* What will happen now?"

A moment later *une baleine* came along *et a mangé l'hippopotame. Et mon père a pensé:* "Wow, this is too much!

56

Diglot Weave

This is the next section of the multi-page diglot weave narrative of "A Hungry Giant."

Instructions for This Page

Have your children continue to listen carefully and follow the story in their activity books as it is told on the tape.

Audio Transcript

Narrator: Just imagine: *Une baleine* ate *un hippopotame, l'hippopotame a mangé un crocodile, le crocodile a mangé un léopard, le léopard a mangé un cochon, le cochon a mangé un serpent, le serpent a mangé un chat, le chat a mangé un oiseau, l'oiseau a mangé une araignée, et l'araignée a mangé une mouche.* That's amazing! I've never seen such a thing."

Just imagine: *Une baleine* ate *un hippopotame, l'hippopotame a mangé un crocodile, le crocodile a mangé un léopard, le léopard a mangé un cochon, le cochon a mangé un serpent, le serpent a mangé un chat, le chat a mangé un oiseau, l'oiseau a mangé une araignée, et l'araignée a mangé une mouche.* That's amazing! I've never seen such a thing."

57

Diglot Weave

This is the next section of the multi-page diglot weave narrative of "A Hungry Giant."

Instructions for This Page

Have your children continue to listen carefully and follow the story in their activity books as it is told on the tape.

Audio Transcript

Narrator: Just then *une main* reached down from the sky and picked up the whale. *Mon père* looked up just as *le géant* swallowed the whole whale. And he *a pensé:* "Wow, this is the first time I've seen *un géant.*"

"Maybe he's still hungry. I'd better get out of here!" And he ran home as fast as he could.

Corresponding Page from Children's Activity Book

Just then *une main* reached down from the sky and picked up the whale. *Mon père* looked up just as *le géant* swallowed the whole whale. And he *a pensé:* "Wow, this is the first time I've seen *un géant.*"

"Maybe he's still hungry. I'd better get out of here!" And he ran home as fast as he could.

58

Diglot Weave

This is the last section of the multi-page diglot weave narrative about "A Hungry Giant."

Instructions for This Page

Have your children continue to listen carefully and follow the story in their activity books as it is told on the tape.

Audio Transcript

 Narrator: And there, as he ate a big bowl of mush, he thought of *la mouche et à l'araignée et à l'oiseau et au chat et au serpent et au cochon et au léopard et au crocodile et à l'hippopotame et à la baleine.*

But most of all he *pensé au géant, et* how hungry he must have been.

And there, as he ate a big bowl of mush, he thought of *la mouche et à l'araignée et à l'oiseau et au chat et au serpent et au cochon et au léopard et au crocodile et à l'hippopotame et à la baleine.*

But most of all he *pensé au géant, et* how hungry he must have been.

59

Story Telling

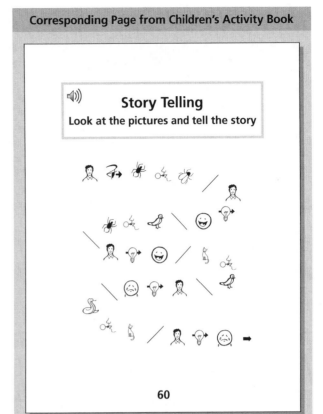

This activity lets your children use the French words they have learned to tell the story of "A Hungry Giant" themselves. The story extends for three pages.

Instructions for This Page

Have your children follow the trail of pictures (from top to bottom) with their finger, telling the story using the French words for the pictured items as they go. The diagonal lines set off sections of the story.

 If your children cannot remember a particular word let them think for a moment, and then go ahead and help them. Your goal here is to encourage them to think as hard as they can on their own, while keeping them from getting discouraged. Encourage them to create their own stories if they like, using the pictures in this activity.

Audio Transcript

 Narrator: Now it's your turn to tell the story. Follow the trail of pictures from top to bottom with your finger, telling the story using as many French words as you can. The pictures will remind you how the story goes, and don't worry when you have to put in some English.

Story Telling

This is a continuation of the story "A Hungry Giant."

Instructions for This Page

Have your children follow the trail of pictures (from top to bottom) with their finger, telling the story using the French words for the pictured items as they go.

If your children cannot remember a particular word let them think for a moment, and then go ahead and help them. Your goal here is to encourage them to think as much as they can on their own, while keeping them from getting discouraged. Encourage them to create their own stories using the pictures in this activity.

Corresponding Page from Children's Activity Book

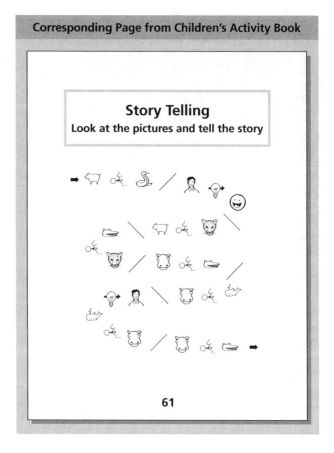

Story Telling
Look at the pictures and tell the story

61

Story Telling

This is a continuation of the story "A Hungry Giant."

Instructions for This Page

Have your children follow the trail of pictures (from top to bottom) with their finger, telling the story using the French words for the pictured items as they go.

If your children cannot remember a particular word let them think for a moment, and then go ahead and help them. Your goal here is to encourage them to think as hard as they can on their own, while keeping them from getting frustrated or discouraged. Encourage them to create their own stories using the pictures in this activity.

Corresponding Page from Children's Activity Book

Practice in French

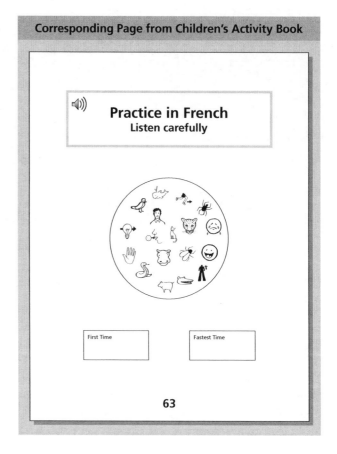

This activity asks your children to tell the story of "A Hungry Giant" themselves using the pictures from the story (contained in the big circle in their activity books) as memory prompts.

Instructions for This Page

Have your children point to the pictures in the circle in their activity books as they tell the story of "A Hungry Giant" on their own, using the French words they have learned. Record how long it takes them to tell the complete story in French their first time, and then record their best time on a third or fourth attempt.

 If necessary, review the story with your children, using the audio transcript provided in this *Parent's Guide*.

Audio Transcript

Narrator: Now that you have reviewed the story, see how much of it you can tell by yourself. All the pictures used in the story are in the big circle on your activity book page. Point to the pictures in the right order as you tell the story. Turn the tape off as you tell the story, and turn it on again when you finish.

Were you able to tell the whole story on your own, with mostly French words? Excellent!

Lost in the Banana Trees

This section contains an audio transcript of the adventure story your children will hear on the tape.

Instructions for This Page

Have your children listen carefully as the adventure story is read on the tape. Encourage your children to take an active part in listening to the adventure story. Ask them to respond to things they hear and have them say out loud words said by the characters on the tape.

 Younger children might enjoy coloring the picture as the adventure story is read. Older children may want to follow along with the written audio transcript provided in this *Parent's Guide*.

Audio Transcript

 Narrator 2: The Adventure Continues: Lost in the Banana Trees

Narrator: "That was a great story, Phillip," you say when he's done. "And this is really fun chopping down all these old banana trees. The stalks are lots softer than tree trunks at home."

Peter: Yeah, it's cool. But I think we'd better head home soon. It's getting dark. We can look for next the next part of our treasure tomorrow.

Phillip: Good idea, Peter. And thank you three for your help. We've cleared enough ground for me to plant fifty new trees! But now it is getting late. You'd better head back right away. If you come this way tomorrow, though, be sure to go straight through these trees. If you do, you'll get right through them to my home and vegetable farm on the other side. But be careful, it's easy to get lost! *Au revoir!*

Peter & Jenny: *Au revoir!*

Narrator: The next morning you, Jenny and Peter all get up early again and set out for the next dot on your map. To reach it you have to go up the canyon again, and climb the ladder behind the waterfall to get to the big bluff or flat place above the cliffs. Then you are supposed to go through the banana plantation to the farmlands beyond. You remember Phillip's warning, and do your best to go straight through the banana trees without turning to one side or the other. But after almost an hour of picking your way through the trees, you finally have to admit that you are lost.

Jenny: These trees are like a maze!

Peter: I know. They all look the same, and they grow so unevenly that it's hard to walk a straight path through them even if you try to.

Narrator: "Well," you ask, "what do we do now?"

Peter: I don't know. We can't just stay here, though. Let's try finding our way out one more time.

Continued from Children's Activity Book, page 65

Jenny: OK. But I'm getting pretty tired.

Narrator: You set off through the maze of bananas again, looking for any hint that might lead you through to the other side. You walk for what seems like hours. At last Peter says:

Peter: Look! Do you guys see something moving in the trees over there?

Jenny: Uh, I think so. Oh no, Peter, do you think it's a wolf?

Peter: I doubt it. Let's see what happens if I whistle.

Peter: See, it's coming over here. It's a friendly dog.

Narrator: "Look," you say. "He likes to be scratched behind the ears, and now he's rolling over to let me pat his tummy. This is a friendly dog!"

Peter: But, hey! Where's he going?

Jenny: I dunno. But let's follow him. Maybe he knows the way out of these trees.

Peter: Good thinking, Jenny, I bet he does. Let's hurry so he doesn't get too far ahead of us.

Jenny: I think I can see a break in the trees up there. Thank goodness. I was afraid we'd be lost in these trees all day!

Narrator: "Yeah," you agree. "And maybe have to spend the night!" You, Jenny and Peter follow the dog through the trees, and after just a few minutes Jenny says:

Jenny: Well, here we are at the edge of the trees. It looks like farmland ahead, just like the map shows. The next place we're searching for seems to be on the other side of this farm, up in the hills.

Peter: That's right. Hey, look over there. It's Phillip again! Maybe he can tell us which way to go. Let's go meet him!... *Bonjour!*

Phillip: *Bonjour!* My friends. I see you have found your way through the banana trees.

Jenny: Yeah, finally.

Phillip: Well, how does your search for treasure go?

Narrator: "Pretty well, I guess," you say. "The next spot on our map is somewhere in the hills up there!"

Phillip: Ah, yes. That is right. I can point you in the right direction, my friends. But by the way, how did you find your way through the banana trees? Stepping through the waterfall takes boldness, but finding the way through all those trees, that takes luck!

Peter: Well, actually, we got lost. But then a dog came by and we followed him here. Is he your dog?

Phillip: I see. Yes he is my dog. And that was good thinking to follow him, Peter.

Peter: Actually, it was Jenny's idea. She comes up with things really quick.

Phillip: And what lesson did you learn from following my dog?

Narrator: "Lesson?" you ask.

Phillip: Yes. There is a lesson to be learned from this, if you could only see it.

Peter: Hmmm. I'm not sure... Can you think of anything, Jenny?

Jenny: Not really. Could you give us a hint, Phillip?

Phillip: Certainly. Let me tell you a short story with a similar moral to it. And you can learn some more French along the way.

Jenny: Perfect!

Narrator: "Yeah," you agree.

Phillip: Let's sit here on the porch, then, and I'll tell you about what happened just last year to a friend of mine.

The Farmer and the Turnip

It is important for children to first understand spoken language, but it is more exciting when they begin to use it, and that is where the learning really takes off.

In this activity we continue with comprehension building, but as the activities progress, we gradually introduce conversation.

Your children will hear a story about a farmer and a turnip several times. They will learn the character names and identify them with pictures. By the time we get to their telling the story, they will have learned to recognize the pictures well enough that they can pretty much tell the story simply by looking at the pictures.

This story is more challenging than the previous story, "A Boy and a Bear," and the discussion of the story on the tape uses more French.

Instructions for This Page

Have your children look at the first page of the story "The Farmer and the Turnip" and listen to the introduction to the story on the tape.

Audio Transcript

 Narrator 2: Activity: The Farmer and the Turnip.

Narrator: The story Phillip tells you is called "The Farmer and the Turnip."

Match and Learn

This activity is visual, audio, and kinesthetic. It is designed to help your children learn by listening and pointing.

Instructions for This Page

Have your children point to the correct boxes and pictures as the tape instructs. In the second part of the activity have them answer out loud the questions asked about the numbered pictures.

Have your children pause the tape as needed to have time to give their answers.

Audio Transcript

Narrator: Before I tell you *cette histoire*, I'll teach you some new words to help you understand. Look at the frame with the white and gray boxes.

Look at frame 1. Point to the seed, *la graine*. *La graine* is in the top white box, right? Now point to the farmer, *le fermier*. *Le fermier* is in the bottom gray box, right? Now point to the turnip, *le navet*. Is *le navet* in the top gray box? No, *le navet*, the turnip, is in the bottom white box, right? Yes. Now point to the plant, *la plante*. It is in the top gray box, right?

Now look at frame 2. Point to *la plante*. It is in the bottom white box, right? Now point to *le fermier*. He is in the top white box, right? Point to the seed, *la graine*. It is in the bottom gray box, right? Now point to *le chien*, the dog. It is in the top gray box.

Now look at frame 3. Point to *le chien*, the dog. It is in the top gray box, right? No, *le chien* is in the bottom gray box. Now point to *la graine*. It is in the top gray box, right? Yes. Point to *le chat*, the cat. It is in the top white box, right? Yes. Now point to *le fer-*

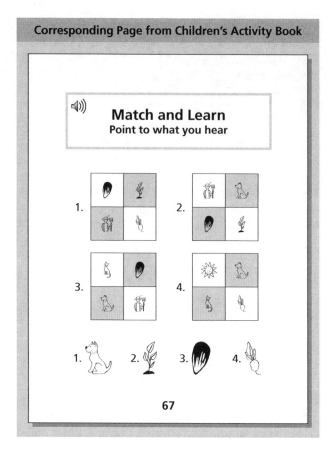

mier. He is in the bottom gray box, right? No, he is in the bottom white box.

Now look at frame 4. Point to the turnip, *le navet*. *Le navet* is in the bottom white box, right? Yes. Now point to *le chien*, the dog. *Le chien* is in the top gray box, right? Point to *le soleil*, the sun. *Le soleil* is in the bottom gray box, right? No, *le soleil* is in the top white box. Now point to *le chat*. *Le chat* is in the bottom gray box.

Now see if you can answer some questions about the words you just learned. Look at the picture with the number one next to it.

Number 1. Is this *un chien?* Yes, this is *un chien*.

Number 2. Is this *une plante?* Yes, this is *une plante*.

Number 3. Is this *une graine* or *un navet?* Did you say a seed, *une graine?* Yes, this is *une graine*.

Number 4. Is this *une plante?* No, this is *un navet*.

Match and Learn

This activity uses frames once again to introduce some new pictures and French words that can then be incorporated into the telling of the story.

Instructions for This Page

Have your children point to the correct pictures as the tape instructs. In the second part of the activity have them answer out loud the questions asked about the numbered pictures.

 As these activities become progressively more challenging, the main objective is to help your children feel confident. They should not be overly concerned with correctness. Encourage them to point boldly as soon as they hear what to point to in the first part of the activity, and to speak out loud in response to the questions in the second half. When your children guess wrong, let them know it's okay and to keep making their best guesses.

Audio Transcript

 Narrator: Did you do well with those pictures and words? Let's try a few more.

Look at frame 5. Point to *la plante. La plante*, the plant, is in the top gray box, right? Now point to *la graine. La graine* is in the bottom white box, right? No, it is in the bottom gray box. Point to *le navet. Le navet* is in the bottom white box, right? Now point to *le fermier* and his *épouse*, his wife. They are in the top white box, right? Yes!

Now look at frame 6. Point to *le fermier* and *le chat*. They are in the top gray box, right? Yes. Now point to *le fermier* and *l'épouse*. They are in the bottom gray box, right? No, they are in the top white box. Point to *le chien* and *le fermier*. The dog and the farmer, *le chien et le fermier*, are in the bottom gray

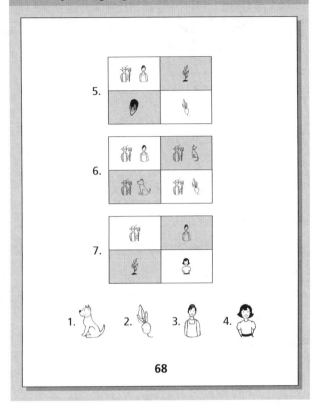

68

box, right? Yes. Now point to *le fermier* and *le navet*. They are in the bottom white box.

Now look at frame 7. Point to the farmer's *fille*, his daughter. *La fille* is in the bottom white box, right? Yes, she is. Now point to *l'épouse*. She is in the top gray box, right? Yes. Point to *la plante*. It is in the bottom white box, right? No, it is in the bottom gray box. Now point to *le fermier*. He is in the top white box, right? Yes.

Now, see if you can answer some questions about the words you just learned.

Look at picture number 1. Is this *un chien*? Yes, this is *un chien*.

Picture number 2. Is this *un fermier or un navet*? This is *un navet*.

Picture number 3. Is this *une fille*? No, this is *une épouse*.

Picture number 4. Is this *une fille*? Yes, this is *une fille*.

Diglot Weave

The following multi-page activity contains an extended diglot weave narrative built around the words from the previous activities.

Instructions for This Page

Have your children listen carefully and follow the story in their activity books as it is told on the tape.

Have your children follow the words and pictures of the story with their finger, so that when the tape says the French word for "girl," for instance, their finger is pointing to the picture of the girl. This kinesthetic connection will enhance their mental connections between the French words and the ideas they represent.

If the pace is ever too fast, stop the tape and review with your children. Be sure to reward understanding and encourage listening. The activity is designed to help your children develop comprehension of main ideas. You may wish to point to the pictures and have them give the French equivalents. Keep in mind, however, that comprehension of every word is not nearly as important as overall comprehension—understanding the main ideas of the story.

Audio Transcript

Narrator: Now listen to *l'histoire* about *le fermier et le navet,* the farmer and the turnip. Follow along and look at the pictures.

Once there was *un fermier* who planted *une graine*. He said: "*Une plante* will grow from *cette graine* and *la plante* will make a nice meal for *mon épouse* and *mon fille* and me." *Le fermier* sprinkled water on the ground where he had planted *la graine,* and the sun shone, and after a few days, a little *plante* appeared.

Corresponding Page from Children's Activity Book

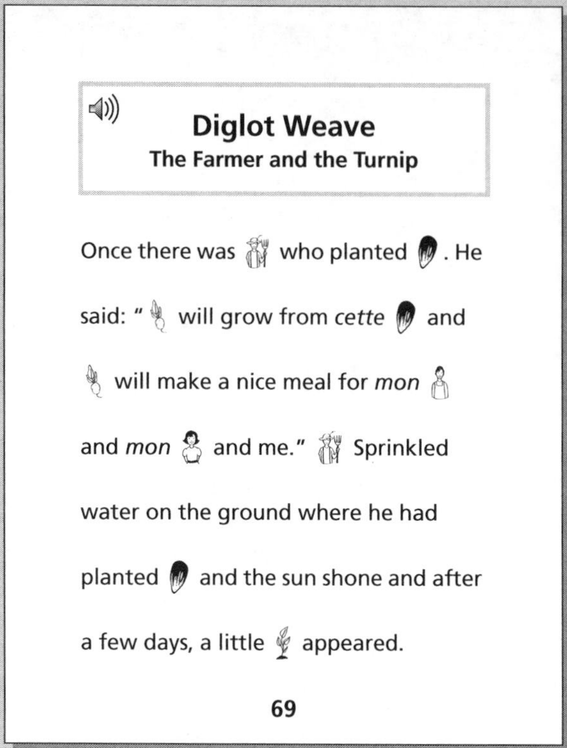

Diglot Weave

The Farmer and the Turnip

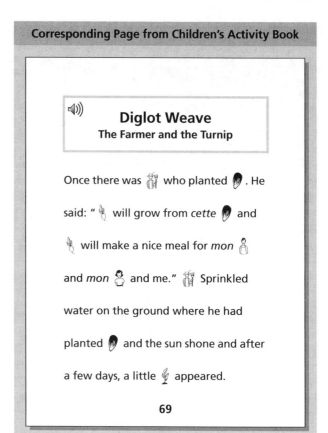

Once there was who planted . He said: " will grow from *cette* and will make a nice meal for *mon* and *mon* and me." Sprinkled water on the ground where he had planted and the sun shone and after a few days, a little appeared.

69

Diglot Weave

This is the next section of the multi-page diglot weave narrative of "The Farmer and the Turnip."

Instructions for This Page

Have your children continue to listen carefully and follow the story in their activity books as it is told on the tape.

Audio Transcript

Narrator: And he sprinkled water on the little *plante* and the sun shone, and *la plante* grew and grew. Every day he sprinkled water on *la plante,* and every day the sun shone, and every day *la plante* grew and grew.

After many days *la plante* was very big. And *le fermier* said: "I think *le navet* is ripe." So he took hold of *la plante* and he tried to pull it out... but *le navet* didn't come out.

Corresponding Page from Children's Activity Book

And he sprinkled water on the little

🌱 and the sun shone, and 🌱 grew and

grew. Every day he sprinkled water on

🌱, and every day the sun shone, and

every day 🌱 grew and grew.

After many days 🌱 was very big.

And 👨 said: "I think 🌱 is ripe."

So he took hold of 🌱 and he tried to

pull it out... but 🌱 didn't come out.

70

Diglot Weave

This is the next section of the multi-page diglot weave narrative of "The Farmer and the Turnip."

Instructions for This Page

Have your children continue to listen carefully and follow the story in their activity books as it is told on the tape.

Audio Transcript

Narrator: So the *fermier* called his *épouse*: "*Épouse*, come here. *Épouse*, come and help me." And so his *épouse* came to help. She took hold of *le fermier* and *le fermier* took hold of *la plante* and they pulled and pulled... but *le navet* didn't come out.

So *le fermier* called his *fille*: "*Fille*, come here. *Fille*, come and help us." And so *la fille* came to help.

So 👨‍🌾 called his 👤 : " 👤 , come here. 👤 , come and help me." And so 👤 came to help. She took hold of 👨‍🌾 and 👨‍🌾 took hold of 🌿 and they pulled and pulled... but 🌿 didn't come out.

So 👨‍🌾 called his 👧 : " 👧 , come here. 👧 , come and help us." And so 👧 came to help.

71

Diglot Weave

This is the next section of the multi-page diglot weave narrative of "The Farmer and the Turnip."

Instructions for This Page

Have your children continue to listen carefully and follow the story in their activity books as it is told on the tape.

Audio Transcript

Narrator: She took hold of *l'épouse* and *l'épouse* took hold of *le fermier* and *le fermier* took hold of *la plante*, and they pulled and pulled… but *le navet* didn't come out.

So they called *le chien*: "*Chien*, come here. Come and help us." So *le chien* came to help.

She took hold of 👤 and 👤 took hold of 🧑 and 🧑 took hold of 🌱, and they pulled and pulled… but 🌱 didn't come out.

So they called 🐕 : " 🐕 , come here. Come and help us." So 🐕 came to help.

72

Diglot Weave

This is the next section of the multi-page diglot weave narrative of "The Farmer and the Turnip."

Instructions for This Page

Have your children continue to listen carefully and follow the story in their activity books as it is told on the tape.

Audio Transcript

Narrator: *Le chien* took hold of *la fille et la fille* took hold of *l'épouse et l'épouse* took hold of *le fermier* and *le fermier* took hold of *la plante* and they pulled and pulled... but *le navet* didn't come out.

So *le fermier* called *le chat*: "*Chat*, come here, *chat*. Come and help us." So *le chat* came to help.

🐕 took hold of 👤 *et* 👤 took hold

of 👤 *et* 👤 took hold of 👨‍🌾 and 👨‍🌾

took hold of 🌱 and they pulled and

pulled... but 🐀 didn't come out.

So 👨‍🌾 called 🐈 : " 🐈 , come here 🐈 .

Come and help us." So 🐈 came to help.

73

Diglot Weave

This is the next section of the multi-page diglot weave narrative of "The Farmer and the Turnip."

Instructions for This Page

Have your children continue to listen carefully and follow the story in their activity books as it is told on the tape.

Audio Transcript

Narrator: *Le chat* took hold of *le chien et le chien* took hold of *la fille et la fille* took hold of *l'épouse et l'épouse* took hold of *le fermier et le fermier* took hold of *la plante*, and they pulled and they pulled… but *le navet* didn't come out.

At that moment, a little mouse, a little *souris,* came by and *la souris* said: "Hey, what's going on here?"

Corresponding Page from Children's Activity Book

took hold of et took hold of et took hold of et took hold of et took hold of , and they pulled and they pulled… but didn't come out.

At that moment, a little mouse, a little came by and said: "Hey, what's going on here?"

74

Diglot Weave

This is the next section of the multi-page diglot weave narrative of "The Farmer and the Turnip."

Instructions for This Page

Have your children continue to listen carefully and follow the story in their activity books as it is told on the tape.

Audio Transcript

Narrator: And the *fermier* explained: "We pull and we pull, but *le navet* won't come out." Then the little *souris* said: "Maybe I can help." At first they all laughed at him: "Ha ha ha ha. You're so little. How can you help us?" But *la souris* said: "Well, we can all at least try one more time."

Corresponding Page from Children's Activity Book

And 🧑 explained: "We pull and we pull, but 🌱 won't come out." Then the little 🐁 said: "Maybe I can help." At first they all laughed at him: "Ha ha ha ha. You're so little. How can you help us?" But 🐁 said: "Well, we can all at least try one more time."

75

Diglot Weave

This is the next section of the multi-page diglot weave narrative of "The Farmer and the Turnip."

Instructions for This Page

Have your children continue to listen carefully and follow the story in their activity books as it is told on the tape.

Audio Transcript

Narrator: And so *la souris* took hold of *le chat, et le chat* took hold of *le chien, et le chien* took hold of *la fille, et la fille* took hold of *l'épouse, et l'épouse* took hold of *le fermier, et le fermier* took hold of *la plante, et* they pulled *et* they pulled *et...* guess what happened? *Le navet* came out.

And so took hold of , et

took hold of , et took hold of

, et took hold of , et took

hold of , et took hold of , et

they pulled *et* they pulled *et...* guess

what happened? came out.

76

Diglot Weave

This is the last section of the multi-page diglot weave narrative about "The Farmer and the Turnip."

Instructions for This Page

Have your children continue to listen carefully and follow the story in their activity books as it is told on the tape.

Audio Transcript

Narrator: Just think, from that tiny little *graine* that *le fermier* planted, with plenty of water *et* plenty of sun, a big *plante* and a giant *navet* grew. *Et* for ten days *la souris, et le chat, et le chien, et la fille, et l'épouse, et le fermier* ate *le navet*. Nothing remained save one tiny little *graine*.

Just think, from that tiny little 🌱

that 👨‍🌾 planted, with plenty of water

et plenty of sun, a big 🌱 and a giant 🥕

grew. *Et* for ten days 🐁, *et* 🐈, *et* 🐕,

et 👧, *et* 👩, *et* 👨‍🌾 ate 🥕. Nothing

remained save one tiny little 🌱.

77

Match and Learn

This activity uses frames once again to introduce some new pictures that can then be incorporated into the telling of the story.

Instructions for This Page

Have your children point to the correct pictures as the tape instructs. Have your children pause the tape as needed to have time to give their answers.

 Have your children come up with frames of their own! These can then be used as flashcards.

Audio Transcript

 Narrator: Here are a few more pictures and new words to learn.

Look at frame 1. Point to *le soleil*. It is in the top white box, right? Yes. Now point to *le fermier arrose,* waters, the seed. It is in the bottom white box, right? No, it is in the bottom gray box. Point to *le fermier arrose la plante.* Is "the farmer waters the plant" in the bottom white box? Yes, it is. Now point to *la souris.* The *souris* is in the top gray box, right? Yes.

Now look at frame 2. Point to *le fermier* pulls, *tire, le navet.* The *fermier tire le navet.* It is in the top white box, right? No, it is in the bottom white box. Now point to *le chat tire the souris.* "The cat pulls the mouse." It's in the bottom gray box, right? Yes. Point to the farmer, *le fermier,* takes hold of, *saisit,* his wife—his *épouse.* "*Le fermier saisit son épouse.*" That's in the top white box, right? Now point to *l'épouse saisit le fermier.* The wife takes hold of the farmer. That is in the top white box, right? No, it is in the top gray box.

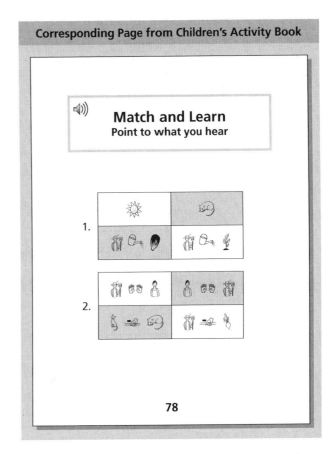

Describe What You See

This activity requires your children to use the French words they learned in the previous activities to describe the pictures they see.

Instructions for This Page

Have your children say the French words for the pictures, or write them on the blank lines to the side of the pictures.

Have your children say or write in as many of the French words as they can on their own. Then you may go back through with them and help them remember those they missed. Continue to encourage them to guess when they need to, and to not feel bad when they cannot remember all the words or when they get one wrong.

Audio Transcript

Narrator: On this page are some of the pictures you have learned the words for. Say the French words for the pictures. Or if you like, write the French words for the pictures in the blanks.

Corresponding Page from Children's Activity Book

Describe What You See

79

Story Telling

This activity lets your children use the French words they have learned to tell the story of "The Farmer and the Turnip" themselves. The story extends for three pages.

Instructions for This Page

Have your children follow the trail of pictures (from top to bottom) with their finger, telling the story using the French words for the pictured items as they go. The diagonal lines set off sections of the story.

If your children cannot remember a particular word let them think for a moment, and then go ahead and help them. Your goal here is to encourage them to think as hard as they can on their own, while keeping them from getting discouraged. Encourage them to create their own stories if they like, using the pictures in this activity.

Audio Transcript

Narrator: Now it's your turn to tell the story. Follow the trail of pictures from top to bottom with your finger, telling the story using as many French words as you can. The pictures will remind you how the story goes, and don't worry when you have to put in some English.

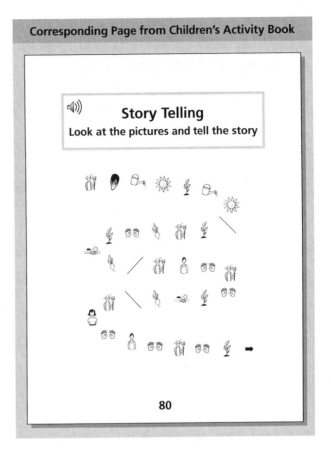

Story Telling
Look at the pictures and tell the story

80

Story Telling

This is a continuation of the story "The Farmer and a Turnip."

Instructions for This Page

Have your children follow the trail of pictures (from top to bottom) with their finger, telling the story using the French words for the pictured items as they go.

If your children cannot remember a particular word let them think for a moment, and then go ahead and help them. Your goal here is to encourage them to think as much as they can on their own, while keeping them from getting discouraged. Encourage them to create their own stories using the pictures in this activity.

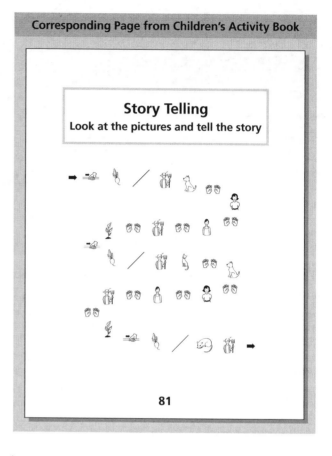

Story Telling
Look at the pictures and tell the story

81

Story Telling

This is a continuation of the story "The Farmer and a Turnip."

Instructions for This Page

Have your children follow the trail of pictures (from top to bottom) with their finger, telling the story using the French words for the pictured items as they go.

If your children cannot remember a particular word let them think for a moment, and then go ahead and help them. Your goal here is to encourage them to think as hard as they can on their own, while keeping them from getting frustrated or discouraged. Encourage them to create their own stories using the pictures in this activity.

Corresponding Page from Children's Activity Book

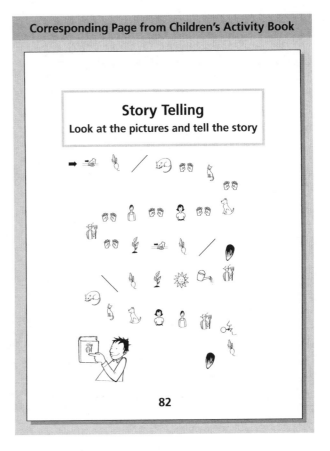

Story Telling
Look at the pictures and tell the story

82

Practice in French

This activity asks your children to tell the story of "The Farmer and the Turnip" themselves using the pictures from the story (contained in the big circle in their activity books) as memory prompts.

Instructions for This Page

Have your children point to the pictures in the circle in their activity books as they tell the story of "The Farmer and the Turnip" on their own, using the French words they have learned. Record how long it takes them to tell the complete story in French their first time, and then record their best time on a third or fourth trial run.

 If necessary, review the story with your children, using the audio transcript provided in this *Parent's Guide*.

Audio Transcript

 Narrator: Now that you have reviewed the story, see how much of it you can tell by yourself. All the pictures used in the story are in the big circle on your workbook page. Point to the pictures in the right order as you tell the story. Turn the tape off as you tell the story, and turn it on again when you finish.

Were you able to tell the whole story on your own, with mostly French words?

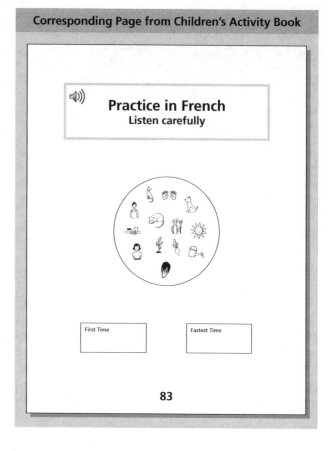

"DANGER" in the Jungle

This section contains an audio transcript of the adventure story your children will hear on the tape.

Instructions for This Page

Have your children listen carefully as the adventure story is read on the tape. Encourage your children to take an active part in listening to the adventure story. Ask them to respond to things they hear and have them say out loud words said by the characters on the tape.

 Younger children might enjoy coloring the picture as the adventure story is read. Older children may want to follow along with the written audio transcript provided in this *Parent's Guide*.

Audio Transcript

 Narrator 2: The Adventure Continues: "DANGER" in the Jungle

Narrator: After Phillip finishes his story, he asks you if you can guess what the lesson is that can be learned from your following his dog to find your way out of the banana trees.

Peter: Well, I think the lesson could be to not refuse help from anyone, even if you think they can't help you very much—just like we didn't know that dog could help us, and your farmer friend didn't think the mouse could help him!

Phillip: Very good, Peter! That's right. Now, you'll want to be on your way now, I think. The next spot on your map can only be reached by going through the jungle on the other side of my farm, right up into the forest and hills beyond. There you will meet the wise potter woman, Jacqueline, who will give you the next part of your treasure. Just

85

remember, the jungle you will hike through is dangerous. Be sure to follow the warnings on the sign at the head of the trail.

Jenny: OK, Phillip, we will.

Peter: Yes, we'll be careful.

Phillip: Very good. Now, best of luck to you in your journey, my young friends.

Narrator: "Thank you!" you call back over your shoulder as you follow Jenny and Peter, who are already hurrying up the trail.

It is pleasant and sunny as you cross Phillip's farm, but as the path winds up into the jungle beyond you come under the shadow of huge trees, and the bushes and ferns start to close in on either side. Before you have gone into the jungle very far, the path starts to twist and turn, and you have to push your way past giant leaves that droop across the path. Sunlight pierces the canopy of leaves and branches above you only in a few places, lighting the ground below in strange patterns. You start to

Continued from Children's Activity Book, page 85

wonder if coming this way was a good idea after all.

Jenny: This is creepy, you guys. These trees seem like sleeping monsters. I feel like they are going to close in around us and trap us here.

Peter: I know, Jenny. I feel it too. The jungle is lots thicker here than it was in the canyon below the waterfall. And with all the trees blocking out the sun, it's really dark!

Narrator: "Yeah," you agree. "I wish the trees and plants and stuff didn't grow so close to the path. There could be strange animals all around us, and we'd never know."

Peter: Hey, guys, look! There's a post with a sign nailed to it by the side of the path up ahead. It must be the sign Phillip told us about. What does it say?

Jenny: Mmmm. It's hard to tell. The writing is small and faded, except for the big word on top that says "DANGER." Can you read the rest, Peter?

Peter: Here, let my try to make it out. Oh! Some of the words are in French! This first sentence says: "Beware of things with *huit jambes*—duck when you see them!" And the next one reads: "Beware of flying things—wave your *bras* if they surround you!" And the last one says: "Beware of sinking places—keep *les yeux* on your *pieds!*" Do you understand any of them?

Jenny: No. But they sound important. Maybe we'd better go back and ask Phillip what the French words mean.

Narrator: "I think that's a good idea," you say.

Peter: Yeah, I think so too. And anyway, it will be nice to get back out in the sun again.

Jenny: Yes.

Narrator: Back down at the farmhouse you knock on Phillip's door. But instead of Phillip, a woman answers.

Josephine: *Bonjour!* You must be the children Phillip met yesterday. He told me about you.

Jenny: Oh, are you Phillip's wife?

Josephine: Yes, I am. My name is Josephine.

Narrator: "But Josephine," you say, "your French sounds a bit different then Phillip's, even."

Josephine: Ah, you have a good ear for accents, my friend. I speak French a bit differently because I am from Switzerland, not France. Many people speak French in Switzerland as well.

Jenny: That's neat. My mom has always said she'd like to visit there. Could you tell us about it?

Peter: Yeah!

Josephine: Certainly, I would be happy to. Switzerland is a beautiful country. In fact, many people consider it the most beautiful country in the world. In Switzerland there are many high mountains and lovely clear lakes. The country is sometimes called the "roof of Europe" because it is the home of a group of very tall mountains called the Alps. Most Swiss people work hard and they are almost always on time to things. Some of the best watches in the world are made in Switzerland. The Swiss people also like to play sports like soccer and riding bicycles. They tend to be very active people and great lovers of nature.

Narrator: "Thanks for telling us about Switzerland, Josephine!" you say. "I'd love to visit there."

Jenny: Yeah, me too. Maybe someday my mom will take me if she goes.

Josephine: You would love it. But now, when you first knocked on the door, you looked like you needed help. What can I do for you?

Peter: We do need some help.

Jenny: Yes. We were trying to get through the jungle into the hills at the middle of the island, but we came to a sign that said DANGER, and then said other things we didn't understand—French things. We were afraid to go ahead without knowing what the sign was warning us about.

Josephine: That was wise. It's always good to listen to warnings, especially if you are in places that are

Continued from Children's Activity Book, page 85

strange to you. Tell me what the sign said, and I'll help you to understand it.

Narrator: "OK," you say. "Here, I wrote the words down. It said: "Beware of things with *huit jambes*—duck when you see them!" And "Beware of flying things—wave your *bras* if they surround you!" And "Beware of sinking places—keep *les yeux* on your *pieds!*"

Josephine: Ah, yes. Those are important warnings for visitors indeed. And I think I know how to help you understand them. Come into the kitchen with me. I have just baked some cookies. You can have some, and I'll teach you the words you need to know while we eat. How does that sound?

Jenny: Delicious!

Peter: Uh-ha!

Body Parts

This activity is designed to teach your children the French words for parts of the body. It incorporates kinesthetic associations, drawing and matching activities in going over the body part words several times.

This first activity introduces the basic body parts.

Instructions for This Page

Have your children look at the picture of the gingerbread man cookie in their activity book and point to the parts of the cookie's body as the tape directs them.

 Encourage your children to say the French words out loud as they point to each body part.

Learning singular and plural forms of French words is sometimes difficult. We use both forms interchangeably to allow your children to identify the body part. They will learn the various forms of words later on in their language study.

Audio Transcript

 Narrator 2: Activity: Body Parts.

Narrator: Here are the words for body parts that Josephine teaches you. As I say the French word for each part, point to that part and repeat the French word. Ready? OK. Here we go!

Point to the cookie's head. The French word for "head" is *tête*. Say it out loud while pointing at the head: *tête, tête*.

Now point to the cookie's body. The "body" is called the *corps*. Say it out loud: *corps, corps*.

Corresponding Page from Children's Activity Book

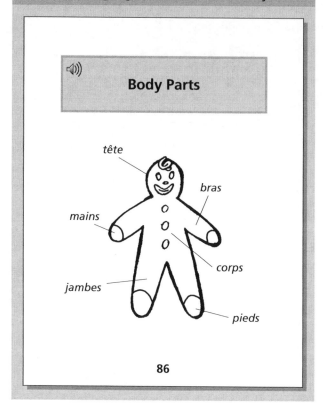

Now point to the arms. "Arms" in French are called *bras*. Say those out loud: *bras, bras*.

Now point to the cookie's hands: its *mains*. Say *mains* out loud: *mains, mains*.

Now, point to the cookie's legs. The French word for legs is *jambes*. Say it out loud: *jambes, jambes*.

Finally, point to the cookie's feet. In French feet are called *pieds*. Say it out loud: *pieds, pieds*.

Did you point to each part and say the French word for it out loud? Good! Now you know the words for the basic parts of the body. As we go along, you'll learn them even better!

Match and Learn

This activity reviews the basic body parts your children have just been introduced to by showing cookies with some parts missing (eaten) and asking them to point to the cookies with the specified missing parts.

Instructions for This Page

Have your children look at the pictures of partly eaten cookies and point to the ones with those missing parts indicated on the tape.

A fun extension of this activity would be to make cookies shaped like people and have your children say the name of each body part as they eat it—a good review and a yummy treat!

Audio Transcript

Narrator: To help you review the French words you have just learned, try looking at the partly eaten cookies on your activity book page and pointing to the ones I describe.

Point to the cookie without a *tête*. Did you point to the cookie without a head? Good.

Now point to the cookie that is missing one *bras*. Did you point to the cookie with only one *bras*? Good.

Now point to the cookie with no *mains* at all. Did you point to the one without any hands? Good.

Now find the cookie that has only one *jambe*. Did you find the one with only one leg? Great!

OK, now point to the cookie with a head, arms and legs, but no *corps*. Did you pick the one without a body? Good.

Corresponding Page from Children's Activity Book

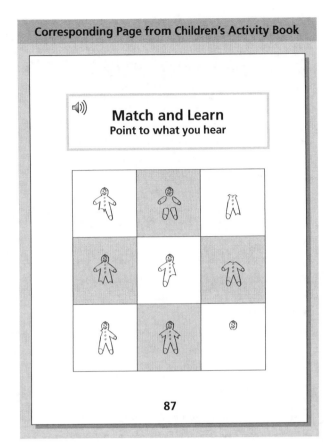

Match and Learn
Point to what you hear

87

Now point to the cookie with missing *pieds*. Did you point to the cookie that doesn't have any feet? Good.

Now find a cookie with only one *bras*, and only one *jambe*. Did you find the cookie with only one *bras* and only one leg? Good.

Now see if you can find a cookie with only one *pied*, no *tête*, and no *bras*. Did you find the one with only one foot, no head, and no arms? Good.

Finally, can you see a cookie with a *tête*, but no *corps* to go with it? Did you pick the one that is just a head? That's the right one!

Draw and Learn

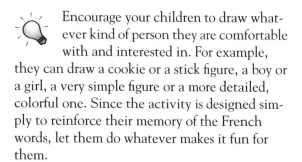

This activity invites your children to draw a cookie of their own based on instructions given using French body part words.

Instructions for This Page

Have your children draw simple figures of their own, part by part as the tape directs. Have your children pause the tape as needed to have time for drawing.

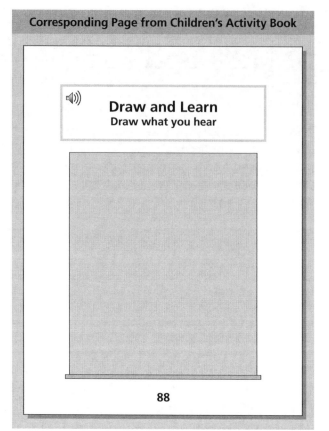

Corresponding Page from Children's Activity Book

🔊 **Draw and Learn**
Draw what you hear

88

Encourage your children to draw whatever kind of person they are comfortable with and interested in. For example, they can draw a cookie or a stick figure, a boy or a girl, a very simple figure or a more detailed, colorful one. Since the activity is designed simply to reinforce their memory of the French words, let them do whatever makes it fun for them.

Audio Transcript

Narrator: Now that you know the French words for parts of the body, it's your turn to draw! Use a crayon, pencil, pen or marker to draw the parts of a person on the chalkboard as I say them in French. You can stop the tape and go get something to draw with if you need to. Are you ready to draw? All right, here we go!

First, draw a *tête*. Are you finished? Good!

Now, add to the *tête* a *corps*. OK.

Now add *jambes* to the *corps*.

And add *pieds* where they go.

Now add *bras* where they go.

Have you done all that? Good! What's left? *mains?* Right!

Add *mains* where they go. Are you done? All right. That should do it!

Now that your person is all drawn, fill it in or color it however you want. When you're done, turn the page to see an example of what you might have drawn.

Draw and Learn

This page contains a sample drawing for your children to compare theirs to, and it also reinforces the French body part words.

Instructions for This Page

Have your children look at the picture of the gingerbread man cookie in their activity book and compare it to their drawing on the previous page. Have them look at the body parts as they are reviewed on the tape a final time.

 If your children need more practice with the basic body parts, rewind the tape and let them try drawing figures a few more times.

Audio Transcript

Narrator: Here is a cookie that looks kind of like the one you just drew. It has all the body parts: a head—a *tête*, a body—a *corps*, legs—*jambes*, arms—*bras*, hands—*mains*, and feet—*pieds*. You can color this cookie now, if you like.

Corresponding Page from Children's Activity Book

89

Match and Learn

This activity tests your children's memory of the French body part words learned so far.

Instructions for This Page

Have your children look at the Match and Learn frames and point to the appropriate pictures as the French words are read on the tape. Have your children pause the tape as needed to have time to give their answers.

 Encourage your children to guess boldly in this activity. If they guess wrong, they will usually have a chance to try again in a subsequent frame.

Audio Transcript

 Narrator: You've learned those French words very quickly. Do you think you can remember them all? Let's see! In each frame, point to what you hear.

Look at frame 1. Point to the *mains*. Did you point to the hand? Good! Now point to the *tête*. Did you point to the head? Great! Finally, point to the *jambe*. Did you point to the leg? That's right.

Now look at frame 2. First, point to the *bras*. Did you point to the *bras*? That's right! Now point to the *corps*. Did you point to the body? Well done. Finally, point to the *pied*. Did you point to the foot? Good.

Now look at frame 3. Can you see a *jambe*? Did you choose the leg? That's right. Now, can you see a *tête*? Did you point to the head? Correct! And last, do you see a *mains* here? Yes? It's a hand right?

Now look at frame 4. Point to the *corps*. Are you pointing to the body? Now point to the *bras*. Did

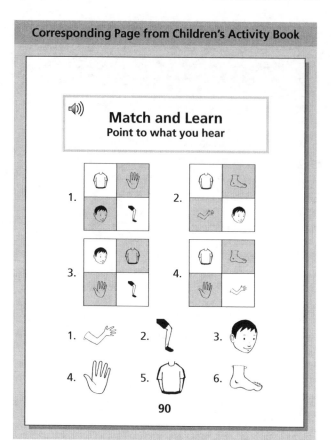

you point to the arm? Now point to the *pied*. Did you choose the foot? Good.

Now look at the numbered pictures at the bottom of the page. As I say the English word for each picture, say the French word for that picture out loud.

Number 1. Arm. Did you say *bras*? Good.

Number 2. Leg. Did you say *jambe*? Good.

Number 3. Head. Did you say *tête*? Good.

Number 4. Hand. Did you say *mains*? Good.

Number 5. Body. Did you say *corps*? Good.

Number 6. Foot. Did you say *pied*? Well done.

Draw and Learn

This activity teaches your children the French word for fingers in a fun way by letting them trace around their own fingers.

Instructions for This Page

Have your children trace their hand in the chalkboard space on their activity book pages.

Audio Transcript

Narrator: Now that you know all those words, it is time for a new one: the French word for fingers. "Fingers" in French are called *doigts*. To help you learn this word, I'd like you to trace your hand on the chalkboard on your page. This is easy to do, and you have probably even done it before. All you need to do is put your hand down on the page right in the middle of the chalkboard, and trace around it with a crayon or a pencil. Go ahead and trace your hand now.

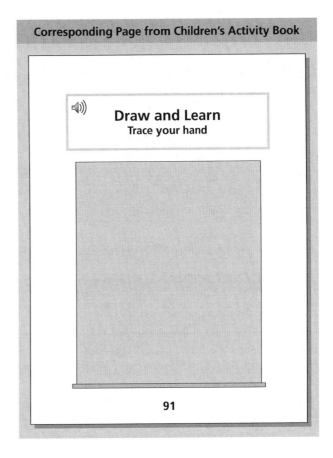

Corresponding Page from Children's Activity Book

Draw and Learn
Trace your hand

91

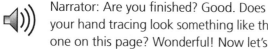

Draw and Learn

92

This page contains a sample of what your children's hand tracing may have looked like. This page also reinforces both the French word for fingers and the French numbers one through five by having your children count the fingers on the sample hand.

Instructions for This Page

Have your children compare their tracing to the sample on this page. Then have them point to the fingers one by one and count out loud as they are counted on the tape.

 If your children would like, they may turn back to the previous page and count the fingers of their own drawing.

Audio Transcript

Narrator: Are you finished? Good. Does your hand tracing look something like the one on this page? Wonderful! Now let's learn more about fingers.

How many fingers—how many *doigts*—does your hand have? Five? That's right! Let's count the *doigts* in French. *Un doigt, deux doigts, trois doigts, quatre doigts, cinq doigts!* Let's count them one more time. *Un doigt, deux doigts, trois doigts, quatre doigts, cinq doigts!*

Face Parts

This next part of the activity is designed to teach your children the French words for parts of the face. The following activities incorporate kinesthetic associations, drawing, matching and singing in going over the new words several times.

Instructions for This Page

Have your children look at the picture of the boy's face in their activity book and point to the parts of the face as the tape directs them.

 Encourage your children to say the French words out loud as they point to each part.

Corresponding Page from Children's Activity Book

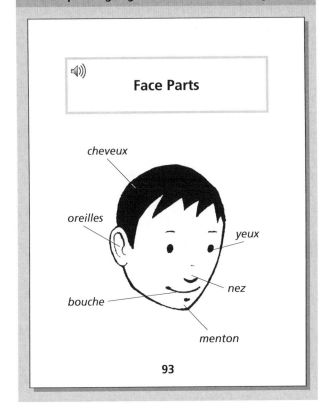

Face Parts

cheveux

oreilles

yeux

bouche

nez

menton

93

Audio Transcript

Narrator: Now that you know the French words for parts of your body, you're ready to learn the words for parts of your face, your *visage*. Look at the face of the boy on your activity book page and point to the different parts as I tell you their names in English and French.

Point to the boy's eyes. The French word for "the eyes" is *les yeux*. Say it out loud: *les yeux, les yeux*.

Now point to the boy's nose. The word for "nose" in French is *nez*. Say it out loud: *nez, nez*.

Now point to the boy's ears. The French word for "ears" is *oreilles*. Say it out loud: *oreilles, oreilles*.

Now point to the boy's mouth—his *bouche*. *bouche* is the French word for mouth. Say it out loud: *bouche, bouche*.

Now point to the boy's hair. The French word for hair is *cheveux*. *Cheveux* means hair. Say it out loud: *cheveux, cheveux*.

Now point to the boy's chin. The French word for "chin" is *menton*. Say it out loud: *menton, menton*.

Can you remember all those? I'll go through them quickly one more time. Point to what you hear. First, *les yeux*—the eyes. Next, the *nez*—the nose. Now the *oreilles*—ears, and the *bouche*—the mouth. Now point to the *cheveux*—hair; and finally, the *menton*, the chin. Did you point to each one? Very good!

Draw and Learn

This activity is designed to reinforce the French words for parts of the face in a fun way by having your children draw them.

Instructions for This Page

Have your children draw parts of the face on the oval shown in their work book as the tape directs them. Have your children pause the tape as needed to have time for drawing.

 Encourage your children to be creative and draw whatever type of face they want, provided the parts are those called for on the tape.

Audio Transcript

 Narrator: Now that you've learned those words, let's try drawing a face. On your activity book page there is a blank face ready to color on. As I say the words in French, draw the things I say on the blank face. Are you ready to draw? OK!

First draw a *bouche* on the face. Are you finished? Good. Did you draw a mouth? That's right!

Now draw *les yeux* on the face. Are you finished? Did you draw two eyes? Good!

Now draw *oreilles* where they go. Did you draw ears on the sides? Good.

Now draw a *nez* on the face. Does your face have a nose now? Good.

Now draw *cheveux* where it goes. Did you draw hair? That's right!

And that's all, except, of course, for the *menton*— but the face already has a kind of *menton*! (You can draw a better one if you want to.)

Corresponding Page from Children's Activity Book

🔊 **Draw and Learn**
Draw what you hear

94

Match and Learn

This activity tests your children's memory of the French face part words they have learned.

Instructions for This Page

Have your children look at the match and learn frames and point to the appropriate pictures as the French words are read on the tape.

Encourage your children to guess boldly in this activity. If they guess wrong, they will usually have a chance to try again in a subsequent frame.

Audio Transcript

Narrator: You've learned those French words very quickly. Do you think you can remember them all? Let's see! In each frame, point to what you hear.

Look at frame 1. Point to *le menton*. Did you point to the chin? Good! Now point to *l'œil*. Did you point to the eye? Good. To say "the eye" in French you say *l'œil*. To say "the eyes" in French, you say *les yeux*. Finally, point to *l'oreille*. Did you point to the ear? Well done.

Now look at frame 2. First, point to *la bouche*. Did you point to the mouth? Now point to *le nez*. Did you point to the nose? Good. Finally, point to *les cheveux*. Did you point to the hair? Good.

Now look at frame 3. Point to *une oreille*? Did you point to an ear? Now, point to *un œil*. Did you point to the eye? Good. And last, do you see *un menton* here? Is it a chin? That's right.

Now look at frame 4. Point to *le main* with *trois doigts* up. Are you pointing to the hand with three fingers up? Now point to *le main* with *cinq doigts* up. Did you point to the hand with all five fingers

up? Very good. Now point to *le main* with *quatre doigts* up. Did you choose the one with four fingers up? That's right!

Now look at the numbered pictures at the bottom of the page. As I say the English word for each picture, say the French word for that picture out loud.

Number 1. Ear. Did you say *oreille?* Good.

Number 2. Eye. Did you say *œil?* Good.

Number 3. Mouth. Did you say *bouche?* Good.

Number 4. Nose. Did you say *nez?* Good.

Number 5. Chin. Did you say *menton?* Good.

Number 6. Hair. Did you say *cheveux?* That's exactly right.

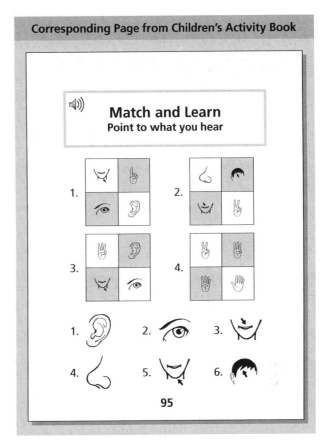

Touch and Learn

This activity tests and reinforces your children's memory of the French body part and face part words they have learned by having them touch those parts of their own bodies and faces.

Instructions for This Page

Have your children listen to the French words said on the tape and touch the parts of their bodies and faces that the tape directs.

 Encourage your children to stand up and have fun with this activity. Encourage them to guess boldly.

Audio Transcript

 Narrator: You've now learned the French words for all the main parts of your body and your face. Do you think you can remember them all? Let's see! Stand up, and as I say the French word for a part of your body or your face, touch it. For example, if I say: "Touch your *tête*," you should touch your head.

Let's try a few.

Touch your *nez*. Did you touch your nose? Good.

Now touch your *bras*. Did you touch your arms? That's right.

Now touch your *pieds*. Did you touch your feet? Good.

Now touch your *corps*. Did you touch your body? Good job.

Now touch your *bouche*. Did you touch your mouth? Right.

Now touch your *menton*. Did you touch your chin! Good.

Corresponding Page from Children's Activity Book

Touch and Learn
Touch what you hear

1. *Nez*   6. *Menton*

2. *Bras*   7. *Mains*

3. *Pieds*   8. *Oreilles*

4. *Corps*   9. *Cheveux*

5. *Bouche*   10. *Jambes*

96

Now touch your *mains*. Did you touch your *mains* with your *mains*? I'll bet you did! Your *mains* are your hands, right?

Now touch your *oreilles*. Did you touch your ears? Good.

Now touch your *cheveux*. Did you touch your hair? Right on.

Now touch your *jambes*. Did you touch your legs? Excellent!

Sing and Learn

In this activity your children use the words they have learned to sing an action song. This reinforces the words in their memory one last time, and makes learning them fun.

Instructions for This Page

Have your children listen to the song on the tape once completely through, then on the second, third and fourth times, have them try to sing along and touch the body parts sung in the song.

 Many children enjoy action songs very much, and they are one of the best ways to reinforce words in memory. Encourage your children to make up their own body parts songs!

Audio Transcript

 Narrator: Now that you've learned the French words for all those parts of your body, you're ready to sing a song using them. The first time through, just listen to the song and think of the body parts that the words stand for. Then the second time through stand up and try to sing along and touch the parts of your body as you say them. Start out singing the song slowly, and then speed up until, on the third or fourth time, you're singing it as fast as you can!

The song goes like this. Remember, just listen this first time.

Tête, corps, jambes, pieds,
jambes, pieds, jambes, pieds,
Tête, corps, jambes, pieds,
Les yeux, oreilles, nez et bouche.

Were you able to follow along? Good!

Now stand up and try to sing along and touch the right parts of your body as you sing the words for

---

Corresponding Page from Children's Activity Book

🔊 **Sing and Learn**
Do the actions as you sing

Tête, corps, jambes, pieds,
jambes, pieds, jambes, pieds,
Tête, corps, jambes, pieds,
Les yeux, oreilles, nez et bouche.

97

---

them in the song! This time we will sing the song together slowly.

Tête, corps, jambes, pieds,
jambes, pieds, jambes, pieds,
Tête, corps, jambes, pieds,
Les yeux, oreilles, nez et bouche.

How did you do? Were you able to keep up? Now again, a little faster:

Tête, corps, jambes, pieds,
jambes, pieds, jambes, pieds,
Tête, corps, jambes, pieds,
Les yeux, oreilles, nez et bouche.

Did you keep up that time too? Wow, you're quick! All right, one more time, really fast.

Tête, corps, jambes, pieds,
jambes, pieds, jambes, pieds,
Tête, corps, jambes, pieds,
Les yeux, oreilles, nez et bouche.

Wow! That was fast. I'm tired—how about you? Well, now you know an easy way to remember some of the French words you've just learned.

Three "Dangers"

This section contains an audio transcript of the adventure story your children will hear on the tape.

Instructions for This Page

Have your children listen carefully as the adventure story is read on the tape.

 Encourage your children to take an active part in listening to the adventure story. Ask them to respond to things they hear and have them say out loud words said by the characters on the tape. Younger children might enjoy coloring the picture as the adventure story is read. Older children may want to follow along with the written audio transcript provided in this *Parent's Guide*.

Audio Transcript

 Narrator 2: The Adventure Continues: Three "Dangers"

Josephine: Well, now. Have you each had as many cookies as you wanted?

Narrator: "Yes, I have," you say.

Jenny: Mmmm! Me too. Thank you, Josephine.

Peter: Yes, thank you. And now that we know the words for body parts, we're ready to head back up the jungle path and solve the riddle of the French "DANGER" sign.

Josephine: Wonderful. You're quite welcome. But isn't it getting late? I think perhaps you had better start back to your beach house now and come up this way again tomorrow. I'll send my son with you to show you the way through the banana trees.

Corresponding Page from Children's Activity Book

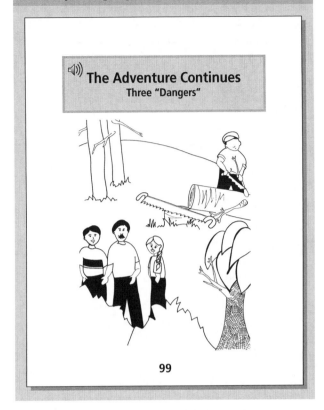

The Adventure Continues
Three "Dangers"

99

Peter: Well, alright. I can hardly wait to go back up the trail into the jungle now that we know how to read the sign, but maybe we had better wait until tomorrow.

Narrator: So you reluctantly turn back, disappointed to put off your jungle adventure for another day, but glad to have Josephine's son along to help you find the way back to the beach. When you get to the far edge of the banana trees you thank him. He says no problem, and he tells you that when you come back the next day you can just whistle, and his dog will come and help you find your way again. You thank him for that too, and then work your way back down the ladder, out through the waterfall and down the canyon to the beach.

The next morning you hike as quickly as you can back up the canyon, through the banana trees and across Phillip and Josephine's farm, and into the thick, dark jungle beyond. This time you push your way boldly up the path until you reach the DANGER sign you found the day before. Now you can understand enough of it to figure out what you

Continued from Children's Activity Book, page 99

need to do—duck your heads if you see spiders, wave your arms if moths surround you, and keep your eyes on the ground at your feet to avoid quicksand. You carefully begin walking forward.

Jenny: Ugh! Peter, be careful. There's a huge spider web right in front of you, hidden in the shadows!

Peter: Oh, wow! You're right, Jenny. I almost walked right into it. Uh! It's really big! And it stretches right across the path! But we can get by if we carefully duck under it, just like the sign said. Just make sure you don't touch any of the webs!

Narrator: "I'll try not to," you say, a bit frightened but excited too.

Jenny: Oh, good, we made it. That was a close call.

Peter: Yeah. Well, now we know what the spider webs look like, and we can duck under those, but we haven't seen any quicksand yet, or...hey, hey, what's that sound?

Jenny: I don't know. It sounds like... like...

Narrator: "Like hundreds of owls flapping their wings all at once," you scream. "Oh, look, Peter and Jenny, it's..."

Peter: Moths! There are hundreds of them. They're all as big as my hand. Now they're all around us! Quick, wave your arms to scare them off!

Jenny: I'm waving!

Narrator: "Me too," you shout.

Peter: OK. They're gone now. Wow, that was something to see. They were so colorful!

Jenny: Yeah. It was scary, but beautiful too.

Narrator: "Yes. And now we'd better keep going."

Peter: Remember to watch for quicksand!

Narrator: "Thanks for reminding me," you say. "By the way, I wonder what quicksand looks like"?

Jenny: I think just like regular sand.

Peter: You mean like that patch of white sand over there?

Jenny: Uh, yeah, I guess so. Let's not get too close to it anyway. How about dropping a rock in it or something?

Peter: Alright. Here goes! Oh, look, it is sinking!

Narrator: "Well," you say. "Now we know what to look for, for quicksand too. I think we'll make it now."

Jenny: I hope so. This jungle isn't scary once you know what to look for, but we'd have been in trouble without the DANGER sign.

Peter: You're right, Jenny!

Narrator: You work your way carefully along the jungle path, until at last you come into a path of the forest where trees grew tall and straight, and it's sunny again. Soon after that, you hear the sound of men working up ahead. In a moment, you come into a forest clearing and find Derek there, working with about six other men. They are using huge saws with giant size teeth to cut down some of the towering forest trees. A couple of trees are already down, and some of the men are trimming the smaller branches off of them with machetes. "*Bonjour,* Derek!" you say.

Derek: Ah, *bonjour,* my friends! You have come a long way on your adventure. I trust you got through the jungle without any trouble?

Jenny: Yes, thanks to Josephine. She taught us how to read the DANGER sign.

Derek: Very good. I'm glad you are meeting some of my friends here on the island. Josephine is originally from Switzerland, you know. And her husband, Phillip, is from France. They are both very kind people.

Peter: Yes, we know all about their countries, Derek. They told us about them.

Narrator: "Yes," you add, "and they said you're from Tahiti."

Jenny: Yeah, is that true?

Derek: It certainly is.

Continued from Children's Activity Book, page 99

Peter: Tell us about Tahiti. Even the name sounds exciting!

Derek: Tahiti is an exciting place. We Tahitians care a lot about *joie de vivre*—joy of life. Our lifestyle is relaxed and comfortable, and we like to treat our guests like old friends. We love to eat a variety of French and Chinese foods, as well as our traditional Tahitian foods. Families are very important to us as well, and we place great value on personal relationships. Many Tahitians are farmers. Our island is a truly beautiful place, both in terms of its landscapes and its peoples.

Jenny: That's really interesting, Derek. It sounds like a really nice place to live, with everyone caring about their families and friends so much. That's how the people here on this island have treated us, too. We love it.

Derek: I'm glad. And now you must be tired from all your hiking. Please stop here for a bit and share lunch with me and my friends. We've cut down the trees we need, and after we've rested and had lunch we'll begin hollowing them out.

Peter: Hollowing them out? Why? What are you going to use the trees for?

Derek: Boats, of course. We come up here to find the biggest trees with the best wood, and we cut a few of them down each year and hollow them out into fishing boats.

Jenny: I get it. Wow, it looks like a lot of work, though.

Derek: It is. Some of the men will camp up here for a few weeks while we work. But when we're done we'll each have a new boat to fish in, and some of the men will use extra bits of wood to make toys and tools and things as well. Jacques over there, for example, is making a cricket bat for his son.

Peter: A cricket bat? What's cricket?

Derek: It's a game a little bit like the baseball you play up in the United States, but you play cricket in a big oval shaped field and the person batting can hit the ball either in front of them or behind them, and the pitcher throws the ball so that it bounces off the ground before it gets to the batter. The pitcher tries to use the ball to hit some sticks called a wicket that stand up behind the batter, and the batter can keep batting until the other team hits the wicket with the ball. Some very good players have batted for three or four days before getting thrown out!

Narrator: "Wow," you say, "that sounds hard to play."

Derek: It isn't really, especially if you grow up playing it. And, so long as we're resting here, let me tell you a story about a group of children playing with a ball in the street, a story called "The Broken Window."

Diglot Weave

This activity is a full-fledged diglot weave story, which means that unlike the diglot weave/rebus stories encountered so far, it uses no pictures to tell the story. The actual French words are used instead.

This story is taken directly from Power-Glide's adult French course, and is intended as a preparation for that course. In order to prepare your children to follow the plot of the story, many of the new words used in the story are taught through match and learn activities before the story begins.

Instructions for This Page

Have your children look at the picture in their activity book and listen to the introduction to the story of "The Broken Window."

Audio Transcript

Narrator 2: Activity: Diglot Weave Story. The Broken Window.

Narrator: As you all sit down to rest, Derek offers to tell you a story and teach you some more French at the same time. You eagerly agree and he begins his story, a story called "The Broken Window."

Corresponding Page from Children's Activity Book

Diglot Weave
The Broken Window

100

Match and Learn

This activity uses match and learn frames to introduce some new words that will be used in the story.

Instructions for This Page

Have your children look at the frames in their activity book and point to the pictures as the tape directs them. Have your children pause the tape as needed to have time to give their answers.

Audio Transcript

 Narrator: Before I tell you Derek's story, let me teach you a few new words so you can follow along. Look at the frames in your activity book and point to what you hear. Are you ready? OK, here we go!

Look at frame 1. Point to the *loup*, the wolf. It's in the top white box, right? Now point to the *chien*. It's in the bottom gray box, right? Now point to the *femme*. The *femme* is in the bottom white box, right? Now point to the *homme,* the man. He is in the top gray box. Did you point to them all? Good job.

Now look at frame 2. Point to the *fille*. The girl is in the bottom gray box, right? Now point to the *gar-çon*. He is in the top white box, right? Now point to the group of three children. Can you guess what a group of children is called in French? They are called *enfants*. Point to the *enfants* in the top gray box. Now point to the last picture in this frame. What is it a picture of? A *chien*? That's right!

Now look at frame 3. Point to the *nez*. Did you remember that *nez* is the word for nose? Good! Now point to the *maison*. Maison is the French word for house. Now point to the *fenêtre*. A *fenê-tre* is a window. Did you guess right? Good! Now

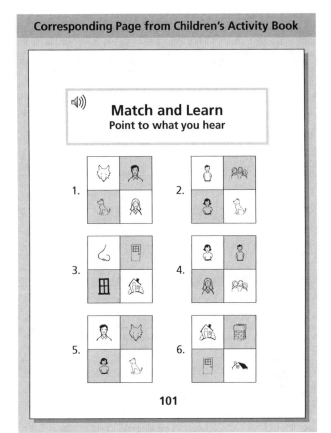

point to the door. The French word for door is *porte*. Say it out loud: *porte.*

Now look at frame 4. Point to the *garçon*. Did you point to the boy? Good job. Now point to the *enfants*. Did you point to the group of children? Well done. Now point to the *femme*. You should have pointed to the woman. Now last of all, point to the *fille*. Did you choose the girl? That's right.

Now look at frame 5. Point to the *chien*. You should have pointed to the dog. Now point to the *fille*. You should have pointed to the girl. Now point to the *homme*. Did you point to the man? That's right! Now point to the *loup*. The *loup* is the wolf, right?

Now look at frame 6. Point to the *maison*. The *maison* is the house. Now point to the *cheminée*. Can you guess which one that is? Yes, it's the chimney. And what comes out of a *cheminée*? Why, *fumée* of course! Smoke comes out of a *che-minée*! Now point to the *porte*. Did you choose the door? Right on. Now last of all, point to the roof. Roof in French is *toit*. Say it out loud: *toit.* Well done.

Match and Learn

This activity uses match and learn frames to introduce some more new words that will be used in the story.

Instructions for This Page

Have your children look at the frames in their activity book and point to the pictures as the tape directs them.

Audio Transcript

 Narrator: Here are just a few more new words you'll hear in the story. Look at the frames in your activity book and point to what you hear.

Look at frame 1. Point to the *balle*. Did you pick the ball? Right! Now point to the *maison*. Did you choose the house? Good. Now point to the *nez*. The *nez* is the nose, of course! Now, last of all, point to the *pomme*. Did you point to the apple? Right! *Pomme* is the French word for apple!

Now look at frame 2. Point to the *cheminée*. The *cheminée* is the chimney. Now point to the *queue*. Did you choose the tail? In French the word for "tail" is *queue*. Now point to the *fenêtre*. Did you choose the window? Right on. Now point to the *toit*. It's the roof, right?

Now look at frame 3. Point to the *chien*. The *chien* is the dog, right? Now point to the *arbre*. *Arbre* is the French word for tree. Did you point to the tree? Good. Now point to the group of trees, the *forêt*. *Forêt* is French for forest. Say it out loud: *forêt*. A *forêt* is made up of more than one *arbre*, right? Now, last of all, point to the *porte*. The *porte* is the door, right?

Now look at frame 4. Point to the *forêt*. Did you pick the forest? Good! Now point to the *rue*. The

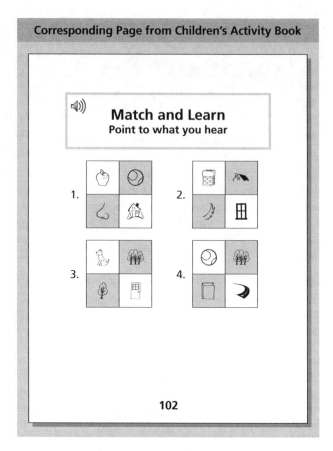

rue is the street. *Rue* means "road" in French. Now point to the book, the *livre*. *Livre* is the French word for "book." Finally, point to the *balle*. The *balle* is in the top white box, right?

Good memory!

Diglot Weave

The following is the complete diglot weave story of "The Broken Window," taken from the adult Power-Glide French course. As your children listen to the story, they will encounter the new French words they just learned, as well as other simple words and some words they have learned in previous activities. The story format introduces the words in a fun and memorable way, and also lets your children see the actual French words on the page and begin to develop their reading ability.

Instructions for This Page

Have your children follow the words of the story in their activity book as they are read on the tape.

Audio Transcript

 Narrator: Now listen as I tell the story, the *histoire*, "The Broken Window."

Would *vous* like me to tell *vous une histoire?* Eh bien, let me tell *vous une histoire* about some naughty *enfants* who were playing with *une balle* in *la rue* in front of *une maison*. In this *illustration*, *vous* cannot *voir les enfants*, but *vous pouvez voir la maison, la rue devant la maison, et la balle dans la rue. Cette histoire* tells about what happens when *un des enfants* throws *la balle, et elle* shatters *une des* glass *fenêtres de la maison.*

Corresponding Page from Children's Activity Book

 Diglot Weave
The Broken Window

Would *vous* like me to tell *vous une histoire? Eh bien,* let me tell *vous une histoire* about some naughty *enfants* who were playing with *une balle* in *la rue* in front of *une maison*. In this *illustration, vous* cannot *voir les enfants,* but *vous pouvez voir la maison, la rue devant la maison, et la balle dans la rue. Cette histoire* tells about what happens when *un des enfants* throws *la balle, et elle* shatters *une des* glass *fenêtres de la maison.*

103

Diglot Weave

This is the next page of the diglot weave story of "The Broken Window."

Instructions for This Page

Have your children follow the words of the story in their activity book as they are read on the tape.

Audio Transcript

Narrator: Besides telling about *des enfants* playing *balle dans la rue* and breaking a glass *fenêtre,* this *histoire* tells about *un homme, le propriétaire de la maison,* who *est dans la maison. Vous* can't see him. *Non, vous ne pouvez pas le voir dans l'illustration. L'histoire* also tells about *une* kind old *femme* who is walking down *la rue* toward *la maison et* looks up *et voit* what happens.

Corresponding Page from Children's Activity Book

Besides telling about *des enfants* playing *balle dans la rue* and breaking a glass *fenêtre,* this *histoire* tells about *un homme, le propriétaire de la maison,* who *est dans la maison. Vous* can't see him. *Non, vous ne pouvez pas le voir dans l'illustration. L'histoire* also tells about *une* kind old *femme* who is walking down *la rue* toward *la maison et* looks up *et voit* what happens.

104

Diglot Weave

This is the next page of the diglot weave story of "The Broken Window."

Instructions for This Page

Have your children follow the words of the story in their activity book as they are read on the tape.

Audio Transcript

Narrator: *Et bien*, now I'll *raconter la première partie de l'histoire.* Prick up your ears *et écoutez! Des enfants* are playing *balle dans la rue devant la maison.* Probably *les enfants* are not aware of what can *se passer. Et bien,* as I *vous* have already told, one *des enfants* throws *la balle très* hard, *et elle* sails up high.

Et bien, now I'll *raconter la première partie de l'histoire.* Prick up your ears *et écoutez! Des enfants* are playing *balle dans la rue devant la maison.* Probably *les enfants* are not aware of what can *se passer. Et bien,* as I *vous* have already told, one *des enfants* throws *la balle très* hard, *et elle* sails up high.

105

Diglot Weave

This is the next page of the diglot weave story of "The Broken Window."

Instructions for This Page

Have your children follow the words of the story in their activity book as they are read on the tape.

Audio Transcript

Narrator: Let us look at some of the *détails de l'illustration. La maison a une porte.* Every *maison a* at least *une porte, n'est-ce pas? La maison a un toit. Le toit, naturelle-ment,* is on top of *la maison.* What usually sticks up out *d'un toit? Une cheminée, n'est-ce pas?* Sure enough, sticking up *du toit de cette maison,* there is *une cheminée. Et,* billowing out *de la che-minée, il y a de la* black *fumée.* What other things has *la maison* besides *des portes, un toit, et une cheminée?* Of course, *la maison a des fenêtres.* From what *vous* can *voir sur cette illustration, la maison a deux fenêtres.*

Corresponding Page from Children's Activity Book

Let us look at some of the *détails de l'illustration. La maison a une porte.* Every *maison a* at least *une porte, n'est-ce pas? La maison a un toit. Le toit, naturellement,* is on top of *la maison.* What usually sticks up out *d'un toit? Une cheminée, n'est-ce pas?* Sure enough, sticking up *du toit de cette maison,* there is *une cheminée. Et,* billowing out *de la cheminée, il y a de la* black *fumée.* What other things has *la maison* besides *des portes, un toit, et une cheminée?* Of course, *la maison a des fenêtres.* From what *vous* can *voir sur cette illustration, la maison a deux fenêtres.*

106

Diglot Weave

This is the next page of the diglot weave story of "The Broken Window."

Instructions for This Page

Have your children follow the words of the story in their activity book as they are read on the tape.

Audio Transcript

Narrator: If *vous* could look through *cette fenêtre-ci, vous* could *voir que* there is *un homme dans la maison*, sitting *à la fenêtre. L'homme est le propriétaire de la maison. L'homme* is sitting *à la fenêtre,* reading. Growing near *la maison, il y a un* apple *arbre—un pommier.* Hanging on *l'arbre, il y a une pomme. Et* on the other side *de la rue, il y a une forêt.*

Corresponding Page from Children's Activity Book

If *vous* could look through *cette fenêtre-ci, vous* could *voir que* there is *un homme dans la maison*, sitting *à la fenêtre. L'homme est le propriétaire de la maison. L'homme* is sitting *à la fenêtre,* reading. Growing near *la maison, il y a un* apple *arbre—un pommier.* Hanging on *l'arbre, il y a une pomme. Et* on the other side *de la rue, il y a une forêt.*

107

Diglot Weave

This is the next page of the diglot weave story of "The Broken Window."

Instructions for This Page

Have your children follow the words of the story in their activity book as they are read on the tape.

Audio Transcript

Narrator: *Et bien*, now let's continuer *l'histoire*. What do *vous* think will *se passer*? Pensez-vous que la balle breaks *la porte? Non, la balle ne* breaks *pas la porte. Pensez-vous que la balle* lands on le *toit? Non, la balle n'atterrit pas sur le toit. Pensez-vous que la balle descend* through *la cheminée? Non, la balle ne descend pas* through *la cheminée. Pensez-vous que la balle* crashes through *la fenêtre? Pouche! Oui, c'est exactement ce qui se passe. La balle* crashes through *la fenêtre et* hits *l'homme* right on *le nez. Oh là là!*

Et bien, now let's continuer *l'histoire*. What do *vous* think will *se passer? Pensez-vous que la balle* breaks *la porte? Non, la balle ne* breaks pas la porte. Pensez-vous que la balle* lands on le *toit? Non, la balle n'atterrit pas sur le toit. Pensez-vous que la balle descend* through *la cheminée? Non, la balle ne descend* pas through *la cheminée. Pensez-vous que la balle* crashes through *la fenêtre? Pouche! Oui, c'est exactement ce qui se passe. La balle* crashes through *la fenêtre et* hits *l'homme* right on *le nez. Oh là là!*

108

Diglot Weave

This is the next page of the diglot weave story of "The Broken Window."

Instructions for This Page

Have your children follow the words of the story in their activity book as they are read on the tape.

Audio Transcript

Narrator: Now what *pensez-vous* will *se passer? Pensez-vous que les enfants* will run away? *Pensez-vous que l'homme* will punish them? *Pensez-vous que les enfants* will have to *payer* for *la fenêtre?*

After *la balle* breaks *la fenêtre et* smacks *l'homme* on *le nez, il* jumps up *et* looks out *de la* broken *fenêtre.* What does *il voit? Il voit les enfants.* Now what *sorte* of *homme pensez-vous qu'il soit?* Pensez-vous qu'il doesn't mind if *une balle* smacks him *dans le nez?*

Now what *pensez-vous* will *se passer? Pensez-vous que les enfants* will run away? *Pensez-vous que l'homme* will punish them? *Pensez-vous que les enfants* will have to *payer* for *la fenêtre?*

After *la balle* breaks *la fenêtre et* smacks *l'homme* on *le nez, il* jumps up *et* looks out *de la* broken *fenêtre.* What does *il voit? Il voit les enfants.* Now what *sorte* of *homme pensez-vous qu'il soit? Pensez-vous qu'il* doesn't mind if *une balle* smacks him *dans le nez?*

109

Diglot Weave

This is the next page of the diglot weave story of "The Broken Window."

Instructions for This Page

Have your children follow the words of the story in their activity book as they are read on the tape.

Audio Transcript

Narrator: *Le visage de l'homme est* red, *très rouge* because *l'homme est très fâché.* When *vous* get *très fâché,* your *visage* gets *rouge* too. Why is *l'homme fâché?* Well, wouldn't *vous* get *fâché* if *des enfants* threw *une balle et* broke *la fenêtre de* your *maison, et la balle* smacked *vous* right on *le nez?*

What *se passe* after that? *Pensez-vous que l'homme* jumps out *de la fenêtre et chasse les enfants? Pensez-vous que l'homme* climbs up *la cheminée* onto *le toit* and then jumps off? *Pensez-vous que l'homme téléphone à la police, et un policier* comes *et arrête les enfants et* throws them *en prison?*

Corresponding Page from Children's Activity Book

Le visage de l'homme est red, *très rouge* because *l'homme est très fâché.* When *vous* get *très fâché,* your *visage* gets *rouge* too. Why is *l'homme fâché?* Well, wouldn't *vous* get *fâché* if *des enfants* threw *une balle et* broke *la fenêtre de* your *maison, et la balle* smacked *vous* right on *le nez?*

What *se passe* after that? *Pensez-vous que l'homme* jumps out *de la fenêtre et chasse les enfants? Pensez-vous que l'homme* climbs up *la cheminée* onto *le toit* and then jumps off? *Pensez-vous que l'homme téléphone à la police, et un policier* comes *et arrête les enfants et* throws them *en prison?*

110

Diglot Weave

This is the next page of the diglot weave story of "The Broken Window."

Instructions for This Page

Have your children follow the words of the story in their activity book as they are read on the tape.

Audio Transcript

Narrator: *Et bien*, what does *l'homme* really do? *Il* throws *la balle* back out *de la fenêtre et* calls out gruffly, «*Les enfants!*» *Et* what *supposez-vous que les enfants* do? *Pensez-vous que* they pick up *la balle et* go knock *à la porte et* apologize *à l'homme? Ou, pensez-vous que les enfants* leave *leur balle et* run away? *C'est exactement* what *ils* do. *Ils* run away. *Ils* run up *la rue.*

Corresponding Page from Children's Activity Book

Et bien, what does *l'homme* really do? *Il* throws *la balle* back out *de la fenêtre et* calls out gruffly, «*Les enfants!*» *Et* what *supposez-vous que les enfants* do? *Pensez-vous que* they pick up *la balle et* go knock *à la porte et* apologize *à l'homme? Ou, pensez-vous que les enfants* leave *leur balle et* run away? *C'est exactement* what *ils* do. *Ils* run away. *Ils* run up *la rue.*

111

Diglot Weave

This is the next page of the diglot weave story of "The Broken Window."

Instructions for This Page

Have your children follow the words of the story in their activity book as they are read on the tape.

Audio Transcript

Narrator: *Est-ce qu'ils sont fâchés? Non, ils ne sont pas fâchés. Ils* have nothing to be *fâchés* about. *Ils* are afraid. *Oui, ils ont peur que l'homme* will catch them. *Ils ont peur qu'ils* will be punished, *sévèrement punis. Ils ont peur qu'ils* will have to *payer la fenêtre cassée.*

Pensez-vous que l'homme a le right *de punir les enfants? Pensez-vous qu'il a le droit de* make *les enfants payer la fenêtre cassée?* What about *la fenêtre? Qui* should *payer, le propriétaire de la maison, le garçon* who threw *la balle qui a cassé la fenêtre, ou* should *tous des enfants payer?* Have *vous* ever thrown *une balle qui a cassé une fenêtre ou qui a cassé* somebody's *nez?*

Corresponding Page from Children's Activity Book

Est-ce qu'ils sont fâchés? Non, ils ne sont pas fâchés. Ils have nothing to be *fâchés* about. *Ils* are afraid. *Oui, ils ont peur que l'homme* will catch them. *Ils ont peur qu'ils* will be punished, *sévèrement punis. Ils ont peur qu'ils* will have to *payer la fenêtre cassée.*

Pensez-vous que l'homme a le right *de punir les enfants? Pensez-vous qu'il a le droit de* make *les enfants payer la fenêtre cassée?* What about *la fenêtre? Qui* should *payer, le propriétaire de la maison, le garçon* who threw *la balle qui a cassé la fenêtre, ou* should *tous des enfants payer?* Have *vous* ever thrown *une balle qui a cassé une fenêtre ou qui a cassé* somebody's *nez?*

112

Diglot Weave

This is the next page of the diglot weave story of "The Broken Window."

Instructions for This Page

Have your children follow the words of the story in their activity book as they are read on the tape.

Audio Transcript

Narrator: *Et bien,* to *continuer l'histoire.* Down *la rue une* old *femme* is walking. *La femme voit les enfants* running up *la rue.* She calls out to them, *«Les enfants! Attendez!»* *Que pensez-vous que la femme* wants to do? *Que pensez-vous que les enfants* will do? A close look at *la forêt* will reveal something sticking out from under *un arbre.* There's a *petite* arrow…*une petite flèche* pointing to it. *Vous voyez? Voilà la petite flèche.* What could *la petite flèche* be pointing to? A tail? *Oui, une queue.* Could it be *la queue d'un loup? Pensez-vous que la petite flèche* is pointing to *la queue d'un loup?* Perhaps…*peut-être…un* big bad wolf, *un grand loup méchant,* is hiding *dans la forêt! Vous avez peur que le grand loup méchant* is going to eat *les enfants, n'est-ce pas?*

Corresponding Page from Children's Activity Book

Et bien, to *continuer l'histoire.* Down *la rue une* old *femme* is walking. *La femme voit les enfants* running up *la rue.* Sne calls out to them, *«Les enfants! Attendez!»* *Que pensez-vous que la femme* wants to do? *Que pensez-vous que les enfants* will do? A close look at *la forêt* will reveal something sticking out from under *un arbre.* There's a *petite* arrow…*une petite flèche* pointing to it. *Vous voyez? Voilà la petite flèche.* What could *la petite flèche* be pointing to? A tail? *Oui, une queue.* Could it be *la queue d'un loup? Pensez-vous que la petite flèche* is pointing to *la queue d'un loup?* Perhaps…*peut-être…un* big bad wolf, *un grand loup méchant,* is hiding *dans la forêt! Vous avez peur que le grand loup méchant* is going to eat *les enfants, n'est-ce pas?*

113

Diglot Weave

This is the next page of the diglot weave story of "The Broken Window."

Instructions for This Page

Have your children follow the words of the story in their activity book as they are read on the tape.

Audio Transcript

Narrator: *Et bien, écoutez* as my *histoire* unfolds, *et vous* will find out *ce qui va se passer. Voici ce qui s'est passé:* After *l'homme* calls out: *«Les enfants!» les enfants* don't stop. *Ils* run away up *la rue, et* when *ils voient la femme* walking down *la rue* toward them, *ils* run off to *la forêt. Ils ont peur de l'homme* more than *ils ont peur du loup!*

Corresponding Page from Children's Activity Book

Et bien, écoutez as my *histoire* unfolds, *et vous* will find out *ce qui va se passer. Voici ce qui s'est passé:* After *l'homme* calls out: *«Les enfants!» les enfants* don't stop. *Ils* run away up *la rue, et* when *ils voient la femme* walking down *la rue* toward them, *ils* run off to *la forêt. Ils ont peur de l'homme* more than *ils ont peur du loup!*

114

Diglot Weave

This is the next page of the diglot weave story of "The Broken Window."

Instructions for This Page

Have your children follow the words of the story in their activity book as they are read on the tape.

Audio Transcript

Narrator: Just as *ils* enter *dans la forêt, ils voient* something hiding behind *un arbre.* Could it be *le grand loup méchant?* Or *est-ce* only *Bobi, un* big dog, *un gros chien* that loves to play *dans la forêt* with *les enfants. Non, ce n'est pas Bobi. C'est le loup. Et il est très* hungered, *très affamé. Il* intends to eat *ces enfants.*

Corresponding Page from Children's Activity Book

Just as *ils* enter *dans la forêt, ils voient* something hiding behind *un arbre.* Could it be *le grand loup méchant?* Or *est-ce* only *Bobi, un* big dog, *un gros chien* that loves to play *dans la forêt* with *les enfants. Non, ce n'est pas Bobi. C'est le loup. Et il est très* hungered, *très affamé. Il* intends to eat *ces enfants.*

115

Diglot Weave

This is the last page of the diglot weave story of "The Broken Window."

Instructions for This Page

Have your children follow the words of the story in their activity book as they are read on the tape.

Audio Transcript

Narrator: Just as *le loup* charges, *les enfants voient le gros chien qui* loves to play *dans la forêt avec les enfants.* «*Bobi! Bobi!*» *ils* cry. Bobi comes running, *chasse le loup, et sauve les enfants. Bobi est un héros! Les enfants* run out *de la forêt. Ils* go right back to *la maison,* knock *à la porte, et offrent de payer la fenêtre cassée.* Now *l'homme n'est plus fâché. Il dit* to *les enfants,* "That's all right. *La fenêtre cassée n'est pas importante.* I'm just happy *que le loup* did not eat *vous. Allez* home *et dites à* your *parents tout ce qui s'est passé.*"

Just as *le loup* charges, *les enfants voient le gros chien qui* loves to play *dans la forêt avec les enfants.* «*Bobi! Bobi!*» *ils* cry. Bobi comes running, *chasse le loup, et sauve les enfants. Bobi est un héros! Les enfants* run out *de la forêt. Ils* go right back to *la maison,* knock *à la porte, et offrent de payer la fenêtre cassée.* Now *l'homme n'est plus fâché. Il dit* to *les enfants,* "That's all right. *La fenêtre cassée n'est pas importante.* I'm just happy *que le loup* did not eat *vous. Allez* home *et dites à* your *parents tout ce qui s'est passé.*"

116

Meeting Jacqueline

This section contains an audio transcript of the adventure story your children will hear on the tape.

Instructions for This Page

Have your children listen carefully as the adventure story is read on the tape. Encourage your children to take an active part in listening to the adventure story. Ask them to respond to things they hear and have them say out loud words said by the characters on the tape.

 Younger children might enjoy coloring the picture as the adventure story is read. Older children may want to follow along with the written audio transcript provided in this *Parent's Guide*.

Audio Transcript

 Narrator 2: The Adventure Continues: Meeting Jacqueline

Peter: That's a really good story, Derek.

Jenny: Yeah, and I think I learned a lot of French from it, too.

Derek: Very good, my friends. And now, hadn't you better get going up the trail?

Narrator: "Oh, yes," you say. "It's almost noon now, and we still have an hour or so of hiking to get where we're going, if the map's right.

Derek: It is. And when you reach your final destination, you'll meet a wonderful person indeed—Jacqueline, a potter.

Peter: A potter?

Derek: Yes. She is a very great artist and as kind a woman as you've ever met. She shapes fine vases

Corresponding Page from Children's Activity Book

and bowls and many other things on her potter's wheel.

Jenny: Wow, that sounds lovely. I can't wait to meet her.

Narrator: "But why does she live clear up here in the hills?" you ask.

Derek: It is here that the best clays on the island are found. She only has to walk a short distance from her home to get her supplies.

Jenny: Oh, I see.

Peter: And she has the next piece of our treasure?

Derek: That's right. Now, you had best be on your way.

Narrator: So you head up the trail, winding your way through tall trees like the one Derek and his friends are making boats out of. You hike for another hour or so, and come out at last in a high valley, where the air blows cool against your faces and there are birds singing in the branches all around you. Not long after you enter the valley,

Continued from Children's Activity Book, page 117

you see Jacqueline's home. Jacqueline herself is seated at a potter's wheel on the front porch. A clay vase is turning almost unbelievably fast on her wheel, and she is shaping it expertly with her fingers. As you approach she nods and smiles at you, but does not stop.

Peter: *Bonjour!* Are you Jacqueline?

Jacqueline: I am! And you must be the friends of Derek. He was up this way just yesterday telling me you might visit soon. Please come up on the porch and find yourselves chairs.

Jenny: Thank you, Jacqueline.

Narrator: "Yes, thank you," you say. Then you tell her your name, and Peter and Jenny chime in with theirs. Once you're all acquainted with each other you ask, "Do you mind if we watch you work?"

Jacqueline: Of course you may! It's always a pleasure to have company, and besides, I have the next piece of the treasure you're seeking, don't I?

Peter: Well, yes, we hope so. But before we leave, I really want to watch you work for a while.

Jenny: Yeah, that vase looks like it's almost done. It's beautiful! Is it very hard to do?

Jacqueline: Actually, it's quite simple. But it does take years of practice.

Jenny: Years of practice?

Jacqueline: That's right, Jenny. Practice is a key to learning, and it's also the next piece of your treasure.

Narrator: "'Practice,'" you say. "That's it?"

Jacqueline: Yes, that's it. But it's no small thing. Practice makes perfect, as they say. And to help you begin practicing, I have a bit more challenging activity for you to do. I'll tell you a story in French, and then you try to tell it back to me. Practice will be the key if you are to succeed. Are you ready? Good. Then listen carefully.

Story Telling

This activity introduces the short story of "The Keys to the Gates of Rome." It teaches comprehension and word identification skills. Your children will first learn some new words, then follow along as a story is told using those new words, and finally tell the story using the familiar pictures as plot prompts.

Instructions for This Page

Have your children look at the picture in their activity book as the story is introduced.

Audio Transcript

Narrator 2: Activity: Story Telling. The Keys to the Gates of Rome.

Narrator: The challenge Jacqueline gave you was to listen to her tell a story using some new French words, and then to tell the story back to her using the new words ourselves. Now let's try together. First, let me introduce the story. It is called "The Keys of the Gates of Rome."

Corresponding Page from Children's Activity Book

The Keys to the
Gates of Rome

118

Scatter Chart

This activity uses a Scatter Chart to introduce some new French words that will be used in the story of "The Keys to the Gates of Rome."

Instructions for This Page

Have your children look the pictures on their activity book pages and point to them as the tape directs. Have them say the French words out loud as the tape directs.

Audio Transcript

 Narrator: Look at the pictures on your activity book page and point to what you hear.

Point to the *perroquet*. A *perroquet* is a parrot. Say it out loud: *perroquet*. Now point to the *maison*. A *maison* is a house. Say it out loud: *maison*. Now point to the keys. Keys in French are called *clés*. Say *clés* out loud: *clés*. Now point to the *lit*. Did you point to the bed? Good. Say it out loud: *lit*. A *lit* is a bed. Now point to the *rue*, the street. *Rue* is the French word for street. Say it out loud: *rue*. Now point to the *place*. Did you point to the plaza with trees and a fountain? Good! That is the *place*! Say *place* out loud: *place*. Now, last of all, point to the woman, the *femme*. *Femme* is a French word for a woman. Say it out loud: *femme*. Good job!

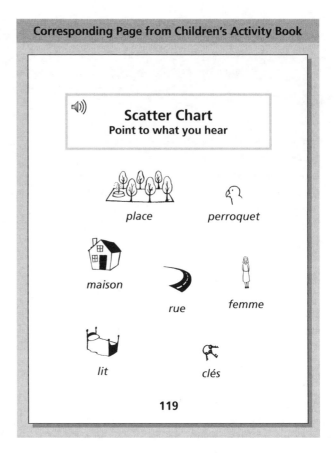

Follow Along

This is the story of "The Keys of the Gates of Rome." In your children's activity books only the French words appear, but both the French and English are read on the tape, line by line. The entire story is understandable because translations are given.

Instructions for This Page

Have your children follow along line by line and picture by picture as the story is read on the tape.

Since the next activity asks your children to tell this story on their own using only the pictures, it is important that they learn the story and the words in it well before going on. You may want to have them listen to the entire story two or three times in order to help them become quite familiar with it.

Audio Transcript

Narrator: Here is the story Jacqueline told you. Listen carefully. Follow along line by line, and look at the pictures that go along with the story too. Remember, after you hear the story it will be your turn to tell it, so pay close attention.

These are the Keys of Rome.
Ce sont les clés de Rome.

Take them!
Prends-les!

There is a plaza in Rome.
Il y a une place á Rome.

There is a street in the plaza.
Il y a une rue dans la place.

There is a house in the street.
Il y a une maison dans la rue.

Corresponding Page from Children's Activity Book

Follow Along
Point to what you hear

Ce sont les clés de Rome.
Prends-les!
Il y a une place á Rome.
Il y a une rue dans la place.
Il y a une maison dans la rue.
Il y a un lit dans la maison.
Une femme est au lit.
Il y a une perroquet aux pieds de la femme.
Et la perroquet dit: Ne dit pas des mensonges!
La femme n'est pas au lit.
Le lit n'est pas dans la maison.
La maison n'est pas dans la rue.
La rue n'est pas dans la place.
La place n'est pas á Rome.
Et ces clés ne sont pas les clés de Rome.
Perroquet folle!

120

There is a bed in the house.
Il y a un lit dans la maison.

A woman is in the bed.
Une femme est au lit.

There's a parrot at the woman's feet.
Il y a une perroquet aux pieds de la femme.

And the parrot says: DON'T LIE!
Et la perroquet dit: Ne dit pas des mensonges!

The woman isn't in the bed.
La femme n'est pas au lit.

The bed isn't in the house.
Le lit n'est pas dans la maison.

The house isn't on the street.
La maison n'est pas dans la rue.

The street isn't in the plaza.
La rue n'est pas dans la place.

The plaza isn't in Rome.
La place n'est pas á Rome.

Continued from Children's Activity Book, page 120

And these keys are not the keys of Rome!"
Et ces clés ne sont pas les clés de Rome.

Crazy parrot!
Perroquet folle!

Now again, French only.

Ce sont les clés de Rome.

Prends-les!

Il y a une place á Rome.

Il y a une rue dans la place.

Il y a une maison dans la rue.

Il y a un lit dans la maison.

Une femme est au lit.

Il y a une perroquet aux pieds de la femme.

Et la perroquet dit: Ne dit pas des mensonges!

La femme n'est pas au lit.

Le lit n'est pas dans la maison.

La maison n'est pas dans la rue.

La rue n'est pas dans la place.

La place n'est pas á Rome.

Et ces clés ne sont pas les clés de Rome.

Perroquet folle!

Practice in French

This activity invites your children to re-tell the story of "The Keys to the Gates of Rome" using all of the new French words they have learned. This effectively tests their knowledge of the new words, and re-enforces the new words in their memory.

Instructions for This Page

Have your children look at the pictures and re-tell the story, using as much French as they can. Have them start with the picture of the keys and move around clockwise to the plaza and then the street and so on.

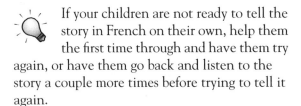 If your children are not ready to tell the story in French on their own, help them the first time through and have them try again, or have them go back and listen to the story a couple more times before trying to tell it again.

Audio Transcript

Narrator: Now see how much of this story you can tell. Look at the pictures in your activity book to remind you how the story goes. After your first telling, review the story before telling it again, even better. And after that, after further preparation, tell it again, better still.

Practice in French
Look at the picture and tell the story

121

Nearing the Final Treasure

This section contains an audio transcript of the adventure story your children will hear on the tape.

Instructions for This Page

Have your children listen carefully as the adventure story is read on the tape. Encourage your children to take an active part in listening to the adventure story. Ask them to respond to things they hear and have them say out loud words said by the characters on the tape.

 Younger children might enjoy coloring the picture as the adventure story is read. Older children may want to follow along with the written audio transcript provided in this *Parent's Guide*.

When your children get to the part of the adventure story where Jacqueline makes baguettes and crepes, stop the tape and turn to the Recipes section at the back of this *Parent's Guide* to find the recipes. Try making some!

Audio Transcript

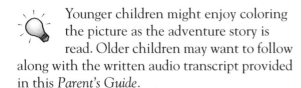 Narrator 2: The Adventure Continues: Nearing the Final Treasure

Jenny: Thanks for telling us that story, Jacqueline. It was fun to tell it back to you after we practiced so much.

Narrator: "Yeah," you agree. "I feel like I know something cool to say in French now. I want to tell it to my friends when I get back home."

Jacqueline: Good! As you practice telling it even more, it will become fixed in your mind. As I say, practice is the key.

The Adventure Continues
Nearing the Final Treasure

123

Peter: Practice. OK. Well, now that makes four clues, I think. Build on what you know, Make learning fun, Don't stress, and Practice.

Jacqueline: Very good memory, Peter. I'm glad you all are keeping track of the pieces of the treasure you've found so far. Now there is just one piece still to go, and you'll find that back down on the beach with Derek.

Jenny: Yeah, I've wondered about that. The last dot on the map is right out in the bay!

Jacqueline: That's right, my friends. Now before you go, I'll prepare some food for you—crepes and baguettes. It's late afternoon now, but those foods are good anytime. And I'll show you how to make them yourselves while we're at it, OK?

Peter: Sounds great to me!

Narrator: "Yeah," you agree, "I'm hungry!"

Jacqueline: Perfect. I'll tell you about my homeland while we make the food, as well. I'm from Quebec, you know.

Continued from Children's Activity Book, page 123

Peter: Cool! Is that the place in Canada where they speak French?

Jacqueline: Yes, Peter. How did you know that?

Peter: Phillip, the farmer and banana grower, told us that people in Quebec speak French, but we never thought we'd meet someone from Quebec here!

Narrator: You all file inside Jacqueline's small but comfortable home, and soon you're busy preparing food while you listen to Jacqueline talk about Quebec.

Jacqueline: Quebec is the only one of Canada's provinces where French is mainly spoken, but almost a quarter of Canada's population lives there, and they are very proud of their French language and cultural heritage. Quebec has been influenced by France, Switzerland and Normandy, and the province is more European than the rest of Canada as a result. Food in Quebec is often a lot like French food, and it is very good. The people of Quebec, who proudly call themselves Quebecois, are very industrious, and the subway in the city of Montreal is known for its excellence. People in Quebec love to play sports, too, especially hockey, baseball, curling, rugby, skiing, tennis and lacrosse. Lacrosse, in fact, is Quebec's national sport. I loved to play it when I was younger.

Jenny: That's neat, Jacqueline. I don't think I've ever played lacrosse, but I'd like to.

Peter: Yeah, so would I. I've seen people playing it on TV, I think.

Narrator: "Yeah, me too. Maybe we could make our own equipment, and play down on the beach!"

Jacqueline: I'm sure you'd have lots of fun. Well, I think our food is ready now. Let's eat!

Narrator: You, Jenny and Peter enjoy your food very much and thank Jacqueline many times for being such a good hostess.

Jacqueline: Well, my friends, you had better hurry back down the path now. I think you should just

be able to get home before it gets dark. You hike is downhill from here, and if I guess right you'll find Derek waiting in the forest to walk with you.

Peter: Thanks again, Jacqueline. It's been really fun being here!

Jenny: Yes. And thanks for showing us how you make things on your wheel, and how to prepare crepes and baguettes.

Narrator: With those parting words you, Peter and Jenny begin your hike back down out of the hills. Derek is waiting for you, just as Jacqueline predicted, and you all walk back down to the beach together. Derek walks with you right to your beach house, and invites you, Jenny, Peter, and your aunt and uncle to a beach barbecue at his house the next evening. He invites you to go fishing with him out in the bay the next day as well, and you get permission to go.

In the morning after a very early breakfast you, Jenny and Peter run down to the beach just as Derek and Pierre are preparing to go.

Derek: Ah, good, my friends, here you are just in time. We don't want to miss the best morning fishing.

Peter: We wouldn't miss it for anything, right guys?

Narrator: "No way," you agree.

Jenny: Yeah, no way.

Narrator: The three of you wade out into the water and climb into the boat, and Derek pushes it out into the surf. Then he jumps aboard, takes the oars from Pierre, and rows strongly out through the waves to the calm waters of the bay. The five of you fish for an hour or so, and as you do, Derek says:

Derek: You three have been great adventurers these last few days. My friends have all been impressed by how quickly you've learned so much French. I wonder now, just how much you have learned. I challenge you to show me!

Derek's Challenge

This section reviews and reinforces much of the course material, using a variety of activity types.

This first activity begins reviewing some of the vocabulary learned in this course. It uses the familiar match and learn frames.

Instructions for This Page

Have your children point to the pictures in the various frames as directed by the tape.

 Since this activity asks your children to remember words which they may not have seen for some time, it is especially important to encourage them to guess boldly and not worry if they do not remember every word perfectly. Also, you may wish to go back to particular sections and review if your children seem to have a hard time recalling particular words.

Frame 5 departs a little from the activity it's based on, "A Girl and a Rat." Rather than having the girl interacting with a rat, we used the word for mouse that your children learned from "A Farmer and a Turnip."

Audio Transcript

Narrator 2: Activity: Derek's Challenge!

Narrator: For the first part of his language challenge, Derek says French words you have learned and asks you to point to pictures of what he says. Are you ready for the challenge? All right, here we go! Point to what you hear.

First, look at frame 1 in your activity book. Point to the *soupe*. Did you point to the soup? Good! Now point to the *chaussure*. It's the shoe, right? Now point to the *balle*. A *balle* is a ball, right? Now, last of all, point to the *roche*. The *roche* is the rock, right?

Corresponding Page from Children's Activity Book

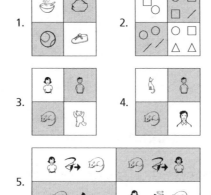

124

Now look at frame 2. Point to the box with *un carré, un cercle, et deux triangles*. It's the bottom white box, right? Now point to the box with *un cercle, deux carrés, et une ligne*. It's the top gray box, isn't it? Now point to the box with *deux cercles et deux lignes*. It's the bottom gray box, right? Now, what's in the last box? *Un carré et un cercle*, right? That's right!

Now look at frame 3. Point to the *fille*. It's the girl, right? Now point to the *garçon*. That is the boy, right? Now point to the *souris*. It's the mouse, right? And what's the last picture? That's right—it is a *ours*, a bear.

Now look at frame 4. Point to the *homme*. It's the man, right? Good. Now point to the *garçon*. It's the boy, right? Good. Now point to the *chat*. That's the cat, right? And finally, point to the *souris*. It's the mouse, right? Well done.

Now look at frame 5. Point to *souris court*. It's the bottom gray box, right? Now point to *souris voit fille*. It is the top gray box, right? Now point to *fille poursuit souris*. It's the bottom white box, right? Good.

Match and Learn

This activity continues reviewing some of the vocabulary learned in this course.

Instructions for This Page

Have your children point to the pictures in the various frames as directed by the tape.

Audio Transcript

Narrator: Here are some more frames. See how many of these words you can remember.

Look at frame 6. Point to the *soleil*. It is in the top white box, right? Yes. Now point to the *fermier*. Is it in the bottom white box? Yes, it is. Now point to the *épouse*. The farmer's wife is in the bottom gray box, right? Yes.

Now look at frame 7. Point to the thing that is *rouge*. Did you point to the cherries? That's right! Cherries are *rouge*—red! Now point to the thing that is *jaune*. Did you point to the banana? Well done! The banana is yellow, *jaune*. Now point to the thing that is *bleu*. Did you choose the water? Water is *bleu* in the ocean.

Now look at frame 8. Point to the thing that is *violet*. Did you point to the grapes? That's right! Grapes are *violet*—they are purple! Now point to the thing that is *orange*. Did you point to the carrots? Carrots are orange aren't they? Now point to the thing that is *rose*. Did you choose the flower? Good! The flower is *rose*—pink!

Now look at frame 9. Point to the *rue*. Did you point to the street? Good! Now point to the *place*. Did you point to the plaza? That's right! And now, point to the *perroquet*. That's the parrot, right? Finally, point to the *clés*. It's the keys, right?

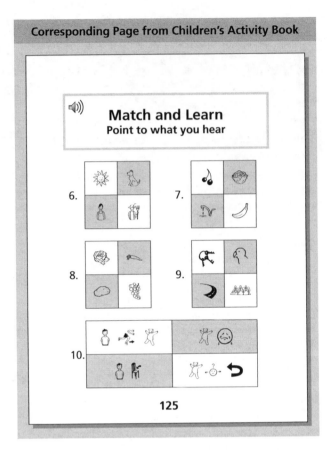

Now look at frame 10. Point to *le garçon s'assied*. Did you point to the bottom gray box? Good. Now point to *l'ours pleure*. "The bear cries" is in the top gray box, right? Yes. Now point to *l'ours hésite, se retire*. This is in the bottom white box, right? Now point to *le garçon poursuit l'ours*. Did you point to the top white box? Good.

Match and Learn

This activity continues reviewing vocabulary.

Instructions for This Page

Have your children point to the pictures in the various frames as directed by the tape.

Audio Transcript

 Narrator: Here are some more frames. See how many of these words you can remember.

Look at frame 11. Point to the *main*. Did you point to the *main*? Good! Now point to the *tête*. Did you point to the head? Good! Finally, point to the *jambe*. Did you point to the leg? That's right.

Now look at frame 12. Point to the *jambe*. It's in the top white box, right? Now point to the *pied*. That's the foot, right? Now point to the *bouche*. It's the mouth, right? Finally, point to the *cheveux*. It's in the bottom gray box, right? Good.

Now look at frame 13. Point to the *menton*. Did you point to the chin? Good! Now point to the *œil*. Did you point to the eye? Good! Finally, point to the *oreille*. Did you point to the ear? That's right!

Now look at frame 14. Point to the *maison*. The *maison* is the house, right? Yes. Now point to the *cheminée*. Can you guess which one that is? Yes, it's the chimney. And what comes out of a *cheminée*? Point to what comes out of a *cheminée* and say what it is out loud. Did you point to the *fumée* and say *fumée* out loud? Good!

Now look at frame 15. Point to the *balle*. It's the ball, isn't it? Now point to the *nez*. Did you choose the nose? Good! Now point to the *pomme*. It's the apple, right?

Corresponding Page from Children's Activity Book

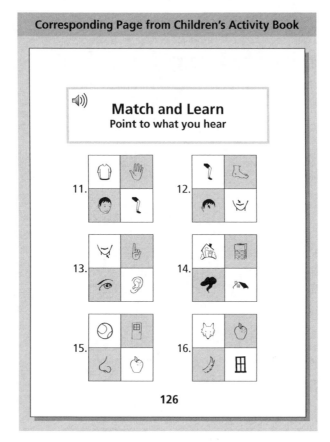

Match and Learn
Point to what you hear

11. 12. 13. 14. 15. 16.

126

Now look at frame 16. Point to the *pomme*. That's the top gray box, right? Now point to the *loup*. That's the wolf. Now point to the *queue*. Did you point to the tail? Good! Now point to the *fenêtre*. That's the window, right? Good.

Match and Learn

This activity tests your children's memory of the vocabulary just reviewed. In this activity words from the entire course are mixed together.

Instructions for This Page

Have your children point to the pictures as directed by the tape. Have your children pause the tape as needed to have time to give their answers.

This activity is more challenging than the previous ones. Encourage your children to do their best and not worry if they don't remember all the words perfectly.

Audio Transcript

Narrator: You did a good job with those matching frames! Once Derek has challenged your ability to remember words of the same kind grouped together, he mixes all the words up and challenges you to remember them that way. Let's see if you can! In this activity, I'll simply say the French word, followed by the English one.

Look at the frame on your activity book page. Point to the *cercle*. The circle. Now the *bras*. The arm. The *roche*. The rock. The *maison*. The house. The *fille*. The girl. The *loup*. The wolf. The *femme*. The woman. The *oreille*. The ear. The *fumée*. The smoke.

How did you do? Did you remember most of them? Good!

Corresponding Page from Children's Activity Book

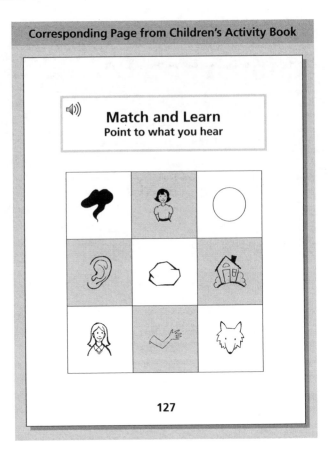

Match and Learn

This activity tests your children's memory of the vocabulary just reviewed. In this activity words from the entire course are mixed together.

Instructions for This Page

Have your children point to the pictures as directed by the tape. Have your children pause the tape as needed to have time to give their answers.

Audio Transcript

 Narrator: Here is another frame. Point to what you hear.

A *garçon*. A boy. A *arbre*. A tree. Something that is *rouge*. The cherries. A *pied*. A foot. A *toit*. A roof. A *triangle*. A triangle. A *souris*. A mouse. A *nez*. A nose. A *ligne*. A line.

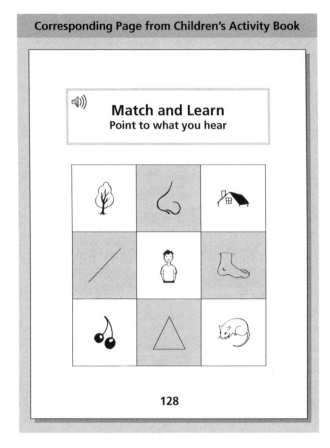

Match and Learn
Point to what you hear

128

Match and Learn

This activity tests your children's memory of the vocabulary just reviewed. In this activity words from the entire course are mixed together.

Instructions for This Page

Have your children point to the pictures as directed by the tape. Have your children pause the tape as needed to have time to give their answers.

Audio Transcript

 Narrator: Here is one last frame. Point to what you hear.

A *carré*. A square. An *œil*. An eye. An *ours*. A bear. Something that is *jaune*. The banana. A *chien*. A dog. A *roche*. A rock. A *balle*. A ball. A *main*. A hand. A *tête*. A head.

Corresponding Page from Children's Activity Book

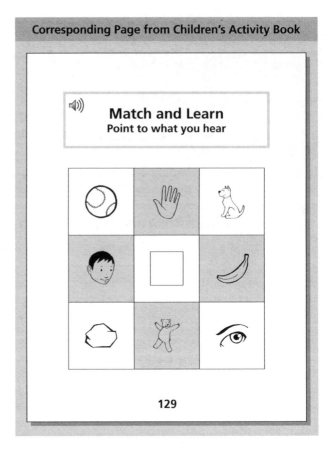

Match and Learn
Point to what you hear

129

Diglot Weave

This activity is a rebus story with French words in small print where pictures should be. Your children's task is to put in pictures in the right places.

Instructions for This Page

Have your children find the page of picture stickers at the back of their activity book. Have them look over the pictures before the story begins, so they know what their choices are.

 Have your children pause the tape as needed to have time to find and put in the right stickers.

Audio Transcript

 Narrator: After you answer Derek's questions, he offers to tell you part of the story of "A Hungry Giant" again, using mostly French words. Your challenge is to put in pictures for the French words he uses. Look at the story in your activity book. Do you see all the circles with small French words written inside them? That is where the pictures go. Take out the stickers included with your course. Look through the them all, then start listening to the story.

Do you have the stickers? Have you looked at all of the pictures? Good! Derek began:

One morning before breakfast *mon père* took a walk and saw *une mouche* that was caught in a spider's web. He watched *l'araignée* come and eat the fly. *Très bien!* ("Good!") thought *mon père.* "*L'araignée* ate *la mouche*. I don't like flies... *Je n'aime pas les mouches.*"

Corresponding Page from Children's Activity Book

Diglot Weave
A Hungry Giant

One morning before breakfast *mon*

père took a walk and saw *une* (mouche)

that was caught in a spider's web. He

watched (araignée) come and eat the fly.

Très bien! ("Good!") thought *mon père.*

" (araignée) ate *la* (mouche). I don't like flies . . .

Je n'aime pas les (mouche)."

130

Diglot Weave

This page continues Derek's story.

Instructions for This Page

As the story is told on the tape, have your children put the stickers over the small-print French words found in circles throughout the story. Have your children pause the tape as needed to have time to find and put in the right stickers.

Audio Transcript

🔊 Narrator: A moment later, a *oiseau* came and a *mangé l'araignée*. "*Très bien*," thought *mon père*. "*L'oiseau* ate *l'araignée*. *Je n'aime pas les araignées*." The next moment *un chat* came along *et a mangé l'oiseau*. *Et mon père a pensé*: "Too bad (*Dommage*); *j'aime bien les oiseaux*."

A moment later, a (*oiseau*) came and a (*mangé*) (*araignée*). "*Très bien*," thought *mon père*. "*L'oiseau* ate *l'araignée*. *Je n'aime pas les araignées*." The next moment *un* (*chat*) came along *et a mangé* (*oiseau*). *Et mon père a pensé*: "Too bad (*Dommage*); *j'aime bien les* (*oiseau*)."

131

Diglot Weave

This page continues Derek's story.

Instructions for This Page

As the story is told on the tape, have your children put the stickers over the small-print French words found in circles throughout the story. Have your children pause the tape as needed to have time to find and put in the right stickers.

Audio Transcript

Narrator: The next moment *un serpent* came along *et a mangé le chat. Et mon père a pensé:* "Dommage, j'aime bien les chats." The next moment *un cochon* came along *et a mangé le serpent. Et mon père a pensé:* "Très bien, le cochon ate *le serpent. Je n'aime pas les serpents.*"

The next moment *un* (serpent) came along *et a* (mangé) *le* (chat) . *Et mon père a pensé: "Dommage, j'aime bien les* (chat) *."* The next moment *un* (cochon) came along *et a mangé le serpent. Et mon père a pensé: "Très bien, le* (cochon) ate *le* (serpent) *. Je n'aime pas les serpents."*

132

Diglot Weave

This page continues Derek's story.

Instructions for This Page

As the story is told on the tape, have your children put the stickers over the small-print French words found in circles throughout the story. Have your children pause the tape as needed to have time to find and put in the right stickers.

Audio Transcript

Narrator: Before long *un léopard* came along *et a mangé le cochon. Et mon père a pensé:* "Wow! *Un léopard* ate *le cochon.* This is exciting!" A while later *un crocodile* came along *et a mangé le léopard. Et mon père a pensé:* "Wow, *un crocodile* ate *le léopard.* This is really exciting. What will happen now?"

Corresponding Page from Children's Activity Book

Before long *un* (léopard) came along *et a mangé le cochon. Et mon père a pensé:* "Wow! *Un léopard* ate *le* (cochon). This is exciting!" A while later *un* (crocodile) came along *et a* (mangé) *le* (léopard). *Et mon père a pensé:* "Wow, *un crocodile* ate *le léopard.* This is really exciting. What will happen now?"

133

Diglot Weave

This page continues Derek's story.

Instructions for This Page

As the story is told on the tape, have your children put the stickers over the small-print French words found in circles throughout the story. Have your children pause the tape as needed to have time to find and put in the right stickers.

Audio Transcript

🔊 Narrator: Before long *un hippopotame* came along *et a mangé le crocodile. Et mon père a pensé:* "Wow, *un hippopotame* ate *le crocodile.* What will happen now?" A moment later *une baleine* came along *et a mangé l'hippopotame. Et mon père a pensé:* "Wow, this is too much!"

Corresponding Page from Children's Activity Book

Before long *un* (hippopotame) came along *et a* (mangé) *le crocodile. Et mon père a pensé:* "Wow, *un hippopotame* ate *le* (crocodile). What will happen now?" A moment later *une* (baleine) came along *et a mangé* (hippopotame). *Et mon père a pensé:* "Wow, this is too much!"

134

Diglot Weave

This page concludes Derek's story.

Instructions for This Page

As the story is told on the tape, have your children put the stickers over the small-print French words found in circles throughout the story. Have your children pause the tape as needed to have time to find and put in the right stickers.

Audio Transcript

Narrator: Just then *une main* reached down from the sky and picked up the whale. *Mon père* looked up just as *le géant* swallowed the whole whale. And he *a pensé:* "Wow, this is the first time I've seen *un géant.* Maybe he's still hungry. I'd better get out of here!" And he ran home as fast as he could.

Corresponding Page from Children's Activity Book

Just then *une* (main) reached down from the sky and picked up the whale. *Mon père* looked up just as *le* (géant) swallowed the whole whale. And he *a pensé:* "Wow, this is the first time I've seen *un géant.* Maybe he's still hungry. I'd better get out of here!" And he ran home as fast as he could.

135

Draw and Learn

This activity invites your children to draw a picture following instructions in French.

Instructions for This Page

Have your children listen to the instructions given on the tape and draw what they hear. Although general instructions are given on where to draw each object, there is no "right" way to draw the picture (so long as the right objects are drawn), and no picture key is provided. Once your children have drawn the picture, have them color it and encourage them to show it and other drawings they make to friends, and tell them what the things in the picture are in French!

 Have your children pause the tape as needed to draw.

Audio Transcript

 Narrator: Once you have finished those activities, Derek gives you some new challenges. On this chalkboard I'll tell you what to draw, and you draw it, OK? Here we go!

First, near the bottom of your chalkboard in the middle, draw a *maison*. Are you finished? Good.

Now, draw a *rue* leading up to the *maison*.

Next, draw an *arbre* next to the *maison*.

And on one side of the *maison,* draw a *fille* with a *chat* by her side.

And on the other side of the *maison*, draw a *souris*, hiding from the *chat*.

Were you able to draw all that? Good work!

Now that it's drawn, it's time to color it.

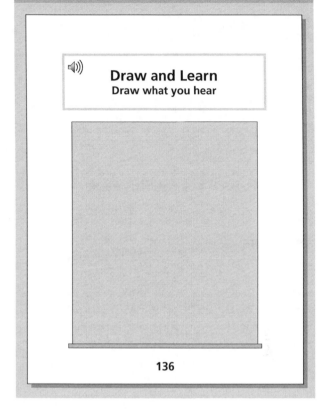

Draw and Learn
Draw what you hear

136

First, color the sky *bleu*

Next, color the *rue noir.*

Next, color the trunk of the *arbre brun*, and the top of the *arbre vert.*

Next, color the walls of the *maison orange*, and the *toit rouge.*

Next, color the *chat jaune* and the *souris blanc.*

And last of all, color the *fille's* dress or pants *rose* or *violet*, whichever you prefer.

Are you finished? Good! Now you can also show your picture to other people and tell them what the parts and the colors are in French!

Story Telling

This activity provides pictures and a plot chain, and invites your children to use the pictures to make up stories of their own.

Instructions for This Page

Have your children remove the Pictograph Cut-out page from the back of their activity books and cut out the pictures along the light gray lines. Once they are all cut up, have them arrange the pictures in order along the blank plot chain on this page in order to create a story. Once the pictures are arranged in order, have your children tell you the story the pictures represent. Then see if they can rearrange the pictures to make another story, and another.

Audio Transcript

Narrator: As the last part of his challenge, Derek asks you to tell him a stories you make up yourselves using some of the French words you have learned. First Jenny tells him a story, then Peter, and then it's your turn. Derek challenges you to try telling a story using French words!

So, go to the back of your activity book and carefully remove the page of cut-out pictures. Use scissors to cut out the individual pictures, then arrange them in the right order on your activity book page to tell a story you make up. Once you have got them all set up in order on your page, tell your story to your mom or dad or your friend, using French words for the pictures.

Any story will be fun! And after you've told your first story a few times, and you can tell it very fast and very well, try a different arrangement with other pictures and tell another story. You can make up as many stories as you like. You might even try

Corresponding Page from Children's Activity Book

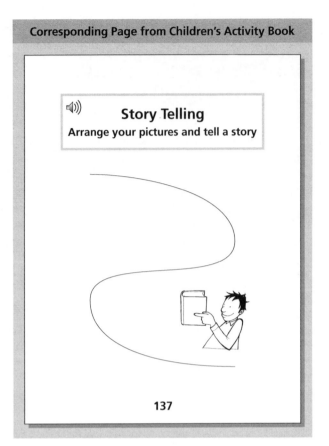

letting someone else arrange the pictures and you see if you can tell a story using their arrangement.

Have fun making up your own stories!

Beach Party with Friends

This section contains an audio transcript of the adventure story your children will hear on the tape.

Instructions for This Page

Have your children listen carefully as the adventure story is read on the tape.

 Encourage your children to take an active part in listening to the adventure story. Ask them to respond to things they hear and have them say out loud words said by the characters on the tape. Younger children might enjoy coloring the picture as the adventure story is read. Older children may want to follow along with the written audio transcript provided in this *Parent's Guide.*

Audio Transcript

 Narrator 2: The Adventure Concludes: Beach Party with Friends

Derek: Very impressive, my young friends. You have indeed made a very good start at learning the French language. I think you now have the tools you need to continue learning French until you someday master it. I'll now give your last clue, the last piece of your treasure. It is this: Make learning a lifelong habit.

Peter: Make learning a lifelong habit.

Narrator: "OK," you say. "I think that makes five now. Build on what you already know, Make learning fun, Don't Stress, Practice, and Make learning a lifelong habit."

Jenny: Good memory!

Derek: Yes, good memory indeed. And now, do you understand this treasure that you have found?

Corresponding Page from Children's Activity Book

 The Adventure Concludes
Beach Party with Friends

139

Peter: It's a way of learning.

Derek: It is. Go on.

Jenny: If we use the treasure, we'll be able to learn lots of good things.

Narrator: "Yeah," you add, "and learning good things is a pretty marvelous treasure all by itself."

Peter: Yeah, it is—even if it's not the kind of treasure I thought we were looking for.

Derek: Very good! I'm glad you found your treasure, and I'm glad you are beginning to grasp its real worth. I hope you'll use it again and again over the years.

Peter & Jenny: We will!

Derek: Excellent. And now, like I said, I think you have the tools you need to continue learning French. This is, after all, only the first of many adventures. Power-Glide's adult French course contains another adventure that you are now prepared to start on. I hope you will!

Continued from Children's Activity Book, page 139

Peter: Oh, we will! Don't worry about that, Derek. Learning French here on the island has been the greatest adventure we've ever had.

Derek: Excellent, my friends! You've done wonderfully well.

Narrator: Back on the beach you, Peter and Jenny spend a pleasant day swimming and building sand castles, and in the evening you go to Derek's barbecue. There you are surprised to see all of the friends you have met in your adventures. They all congratulate you on the French you have learned, and invite you to return and visit them again soon. You're sure that you will.

Quiche Lorraine

1 9-inch unbaked pie crust

1 c shredded Swiss cheese

6 slices bacon

1 small onion, chopped

1/2 green pepper, chopped

3 eggs, slightly beaten

1 c evaporated milk or light cream

1/2 t lemon peel

1/2 t salt

dash pepper

1/4 t dry mustard

Cook bacon. Reserve 2 T bacon fat. Crumble bacon and set aside. Cook onion in reserved bacon fat until tender and browned. Set aside.

Line unbaked pie crust with foil. Put dry beans or other lightweight item in bottom of pan to prevent large air pockets from forming in crust. Bake unpricked pie crust in 475 degree oven for 5 minutes. Remove from oven. Arrange cheese, bacon, onion, and pepper in bottom of crust.

Combine eggs, cream, lemon peel, salt, pepper, and mustard. Pour over cheese mixture in crust. Bake at 325° F for 45 minutes or until set. Remove from oven. Let stand about 10 minutes before serving. Cut quiche into 6 servings to serve. Makes 6 servings.

Les Frites—French Fries

4 potatoes

oil for deep frying

seasoned salt

Cut pared potatoes lengthwise in strips. Fry small amounts at a time in hot oil (360°F) for 6-7 minutes or until crisp and golden. Drain on paper towels. Sprinkle with seasoned salt and serve at once. Makes 8-12 servings. Note: Do not French-fry new potatoes.

Baguettes—French Bread

2 packages active dry yeast

1/2 c warm water

1 T salt

2 c lukewarm water

7 to 7 1/2 c flour, sifted

1 egg white

Soften yeast in warm water (110º F). Combine salt and lukewarm water; beat in 2 cups flour. Add softened yeast. Stir in 4 1/2 to 5 cups flour, or enough to make mderately stiff dough. Turn out dough on lightly floured surface. Knead 10 to 15 minutes, working in remaining flour.

Place in greased bowl. Turn dough once to grease surface. Cover and let rise till double (about 1 hour). Punch down; let rise again till double (30-45 minutes). Turn out dough on floured surface and divide into two portions. Cover; let rest 10 minutes. Roll each portion into 15x12-inch rectangle. Roll up tightly, beginning at long side, sealing well as you roll. Taper ends, if desired.

Place each loaf seam-side down on greased baking sheet sprinkled with cornmeal. Use a sharp knifeto slash tops of loaves diagonally every 2 1/2 inches, 1/4 inch deep. Beat egg white till foamy; add 1 tablespoon water. Brush mixture over tops and sides of loaves. Or, for crisp crust, brush just with water. Cover with a damp cloth. Keep the cloth from touching loaves by draping it over inverted glasses. Let rise till double (1 to 1 1/4 hours). Bake at 375º F till light brown, about 20 minutes. Brush again with egg white mixture or water. Bake 15 to 20 minutes or till done. Cool. Makes two loaves.

Crepes

1 c flour

1 c skim milk

1 t sugar

3 eggs

1/3 stick of butter

pinch of salt

1 t vanilla

1/2 t rum extract (optional)

Mix everything in a blender until it makes smooth batter (about 30 seconds). In a very hot pan, spread a thin layer of batter. Cook 20 seconds on each side.